TREASURY OF BLACK QUOTATIONS

BY

DONNIE E. WILSON

Authors Choice Press

New York Lincoln Shanghai

<u>**DEDICATION**</u>

To my wife, Antoinette, who never lost faith in me,
and to my brother and sister-in-law, James C. and
Carol Wilson, for their enduring faith in the merits
of this project.

Treasury of Black Quotations

Authors Choice Press
an imprint of iUniverse, Inc.

For information address:
iUniverse, Inc.
2021 Pine Lake Road, Suite 100
Lincoln, NE 68512
www.iuniverse.com

Originally published by Interfair Press

Cover by James C. Wilson

First Edition

ISBN: 0-595-32621-8

Printed in the United States of America

ACKNOWLEDGEMENTS

I wish to express my sincere thanks to the following

libraries for their invaluable assistance in this project:

Library of Congress
Moorland-Spingarn Research Center, Howard University
Schomberg Collections, New York Public Library
Enoch Pratt Free Library, Baltimore, Maryland
Fairfax County Virginia Public Library
Prince Georges County Maryland Public Library
District of Columbia Public Library
Morgan State University, Davis Collection, Baltimore, Maryland
Dillard University, New Orleans, Louisiana
Xavier University, New Orleans, Louisiana
Southern University, Baton Rouge, Louisiana
University of Arkansas, Pine Bluff, Arkansas
New Orleans Public Library, New Orleans, Louisiana

The lines from Black People on page 14 are from the book "Some Time Ago" by Chester Higgins jr. and Orde Coombs. Copyright 1980. Reprinted by permission of Anchor/Press Doubleday.

Acknowledgements will be made in future additions for any works not acknowleged in this edition.

THE STRUGGLE IS MY LIFE

------NELSON MANDELA

CONTENTS

PREFACE TO THE FIRST EDITION

This project grew out of my awareness of the almost total disregard for Blacks in works of quotations. This omission is clearly a travesty of justice. Moreover, as this book goes to press, Black people are besieged by soaring unemployment, Black on Black crime, drug abuse, teenage pregnancy, and a pernicious assault by the establishment on civil rights gains made during the 1960's and 1970's. Black people have always persevered because of an indomitable will to endure. I have no doubt that they will continue to survive; however, the issue to be resolved is what will be the essence of that existence. For if the present portends the future state of affairs, we are, indeed, destined for a wretched future. The foundation for this doubt is rooted in the seemingly disregard for the values that are at the heart of the Black experience. Visionaries such as Paul Robeson, W.E.B. Dubois, Martin Luther King Jr., Frederick Douglass, Harriett Tubman, and other nameless valiant men and women of infinite resolve, must be weeping for their posterity.

It is my hope that a gleam of hope will result from reading this book by drawing upon the spiritual inspiration of men and women who have struggled with life's vicissitudes.

-----DONNIE E. WILSON

CATEGORY HEADINGS

ACHIEVEMENT

You don't achieve anything by playing it safe.

--Shirley Chisholm

————

Negroes must earn their way to higher achievement. They can't get it by throwing rocks, preaching anarchy or making demands that go beyond reason.

--Thurgood Marshall

* * *

ACHIEVER

Any child can be a real achiever.

--Marva Collins

* * *

ACTING

Films make me into some cheap turn. . . . you bet they will never let me play a part in a film in which a Negro is on top.

--Paul Robeson

————

I find I cannot portray the life nor express the living hopes and aspirations of the struggling people from which I come.

--Paul Robeson

* * *

ACTION

Stop squawking and do something to justify your existence.

--Bill "Bojangles" Robinson

———

For every action we take to realize ourselves, we fulfill the will of God, and His will is everlasting.

--Anwar el-Sadat

* * *

ADVANCEMENT

He who does not advance recedes.

--African Proverb

* * *

ADVERSITY

Adversity is the best teacher, for those who do not listen.

--African Proverb

———

Adversity tries virtue.

--African Proverb

———

Adversity often leads to prosperity.

--African Proverb

* * *

AFRICA

He who has drank of African waters will drink again.

--African Proverb

What is Africa to me;
Copper sun or scarlet sea,
Jungle star or jungle track,
Strong bronzed men, or regal black women from whose loins
I sprang.

--Countee Cullen

Africa has become the big game of the nation hunters. Today
Africa looms as the greatest commercial, industrial and political
prize of the world.

--Marcus Garvey

I learned that along with the towering achievements of the
cultures in ancient China there stood the culture of Africa,
unseen and denied by the imperialist looters of Africa's material
wealth.

--Paul Robeson

I discovered Africa in London. That discovery--back in the
twenties--profoundly influenced my life. Like most of Africa's
children in America, I had known little about the land of our
fathers. But in England, where my career as an actor and singer
took me, I came to know many Africans.

--Paul Robeson

In my music, my plays, my films, I want always to carry this central idea; to be African.
Multitudes of men have died for less worthy ideas; it is even more imminently worth living for.

--Paul Robeson

*   *   *

AFRICAN

The African race is an Indian rubber ball; the harder you dash it to the ground, the higher it will rise.

--African Proverb

*   *   *

AGITATION

Don't stir up dry manure.

--Creole Slave Proverb

*   *   *

ALIENATION

This depthless alienation from oneself and one's people is, in sum, the American experience.

--James Baldwin

———

With few exceptions, millions of Negroes live and die feeling unwanted in this country.

--Daisy Bates

———

As things stand today, even the luckiest Negro must always feel alien in the country to which he is more truly indigenous than 90 per cent of his white "compatriots".

--Paul Robeson

* * *

ALIVE

It's good to be alive.

--Roy Campanella

* * *

AMERICA

We cannot forget that America was built on Africa.

--W.E.B. Dubois

———

Let America be America again.
Let it be the dream it use to be.
Let it be the pioneer on the plain
Seeking a home where he himself is free.
        (America never was America to me)

--Langston Hughes

———

I, too, sing America
I am the dark brother.
They send me to eat in the kitchen
When company comes,
But I laugh,
And eat well,
And grow strong.

--Langston Hughes

———

It ain't our government, but it's our country.

--Jesse Jackson

———

America must be a nation in which its multiracial people are partners in power.

--Martin Luther King, Jr.

* * *

AMERICAN

If I may be pardoned for a personal reference, I am proud to be an American and I am proud of my origin.

--Ralph Bunche

* * *

AMERICANS

Americans want to believe a great many things about themselves which are not true.

--James Baldwin

The whole difficulty in this situation is the fact that the Negro is acting like the rest of the Americans' and the rest of the Americans wonder why and resent it.

--Robert C. Weaver

* * *

ANCESTRY

My father was a creole, his father a Negro, and his father a monkey; my family it seems, begins where yours left off.

--Alexandre Dumas pére
The response to individual who asked
with a sneer who his father was.

My ancestors in Africa reckoned sound of major importance;
they were all great talkers, and where writing was unknown, folk
tales and an oral tradition kept the ears rather than the eyes
sharpened. I am the same way, I always hear, I seldom see. I
hear my way through the world.

                                                    --Paul Robeson

                          *   *   *

ANCIENT

Ancient things remain in the ear.

                                            --African Proverb

                          *   *   *

ANGER

A soft answer is a specific cure for anger.

                                        --African Proverb

                          *   *   *

APPRECIATION

I always appreciate what people do for me.

                                            --Eubie Blake

                          *   *   *

ARTIST

To my mind it is the duty of the younger Negro artist . . . to change through the force of his art that old whispering "I want to be white" hidden in the aspirations of his people, to "Why should I want to be white? I am a Negro--and beautiful!"

--Langston Hughes

* * *

ASPIRATIONS

Don't hang your basket higher than you can reach.

--African Proverb

* * *

ASSOCIATION

When you eat with the devil, see that your spoon is long.

--Creole Slave Proverb

* * *

ATOMIC BOMB

The great danger in the world is not the atomic bomb--it is the bomb in the souls of men.

--Martin Luther King Jr.

* * *

AUDACITY

I have the audacity to believe that people everywhere can have three meals a day for their tired bodies, education and culture for their minds, and dignity, equality and freedom for their spirits.

--Martin Luther King Jr.

* * *

B

BACHELOR

There's a funny smell in a bachelor's house.

--African Proverb

*   *   *

BARRIERS

Once the color bar falls, the magic evaporates, and when the
black man starts to excel in a particular sport, the question
starts floating around: 'Is boxing dying?' 'What happened to
football?' 'What is basketball coming to?'

--Eldridge Cleaver

*   *   *

BEAUTY

He who marries beauty marries trouble.

--African Proverb

Beauty is only skin deep
But ugly goes to the bone.

--Black Saying

_____

Black is beautiful.

--Black Saying

_____

One looks for beauty in all things because all things come
from the creator of beauty.

--Adam Clayton Powell Jr.

* * *

BEGGARS

Beggars do not devour one another.

--African Proverb

_____

We are a race of beggars. Other races, other groups, demand
and get.

--The Spokesman Magazine

* * *

BELIEF

A man can make what he wants of himself. If he truly believes
that he must be ready for hard work and many hard breaks along the
way.

--Thurgood Marshall

* * *

BENEVOLENCE

It is a mighty fine thing to put your head on a pillow at night and realize you've done something good.

--Marion Anderson

*　*　*

BEQUEST

Some folks leave their brains to science
But when I go I am leaving my mouth
It's the greatest.

--Muhammad Ali

*　*　*

BLACK

Blacker the berry the sweeter the juice.

--Black Saying

———

I am Black
   Poushkin or Dumas or Toussaint L'ouverture
   I am Black

--Edwin J. Morgan

*　*　*

BLACK BABY

I have plucked you from the skies
Baby, for my paradise!
Tiny fingers God but knows
How you antedate lifes woes.

Was it fair that you should be
Peon to my misery.
That one hour you might rest
Cuddled solace on my breast?

--Opportunity Magazine

_____

The baby I hold in my arms is a black baby.
I toil, and I cannot always cuddle him.
I place him on the ground at my feet.

--Anita Scott Coleman

* * *

BLACK MEN

What black men do to each other makes God laugh.

--Creole Slave Proverb

_____

They have dreamed as young men dream
of glory, love and power;
They have hoped as youth will
hope of life's sun-minted hour.

They have seen as others saw
Their bubbles burst in air,
And they have learned to live it down
As though they did not care.

--Georgia Douglas Johnson

_____

You're the sugar in my coffee, the jelly in my roll.

--Ma Rainey

_____

Black men in America must speak for themselves; no outside
tongue, however gifted with eloquence, can tell their story.

--Thomas Hamilton

* * *

BLACK PEOPLE

And all the centuries passed.
And they became a kind of people that the world had never known--
hybrids of the west, bastards in a world that sanctioned
legitimacy.

In the center of themselves they alone bore their suffering while
the world theorized about their humanity or gazed on them with icy
disdain.

Now nothing--No gestures, no greetings, no embraces--can remove
the blot of slavery on this nation founded in liberty. For no
black man, however brillant his victory against the forces that
would limit him, can forget the years of American debasement.
"What's gone and past help, should be past grief." Indeed. But
not past action. And as this country rides into its third
century, may the sons and daughters of this country's former serfs
find in the fullness of their lives, a vigorous wisdom that lies
beyond retaliation or despair.

--Orde Coombs

_____

   For my people thronging 47th Street in Chicago and Lennox
Avenue in New York and Rampart Street in New Orleans, lost
disinherited dispossessed and happy people filling the cabarets
and taverns and other peoples pockets.

--Margaret Walker

*   *   *

BLACK POWER

What we gonna start saying now is black power.

--Stokely Carmichael

*   *   *

BLACK WOMAN

Mademoiselle from Armentiers, parlez-vous,
Mademoiselle from Armentiers, parlez-vous,
I wouldn't give my high-brown belle,
For every mademoiselle dis side of hell--
Inky Dinky, parlez-vous.

                              --Sung by Black Soldiers
                                During World War I

                    _____

    There is a kind of strength that is almost frightening in
Black Women. It's as if a steel rod run right through the head
down to the feet. And I believe that we have to thank Black Women
not only for keeping the Black family alive, but also, the white
family. Because Black women have nursed a nation of strangers.
For hundreds of years, they literally nursed babies at their
breasts who they knew, when they grew up, would rape their
daughters and kill their sons.

                                        --Maya Angelou

                    _____

Ah! dear jewel of mahogany,
I love you
As the hog loves mud.

                                        --Creole Slave Song

                    _____

Black diamonds are her bright, black eyes,
Her teeth and lillies are alike.
Sing, fellows, for my true love, and
The water with the long oar strike.

                                        --Creole Slave Song

                    _____

Daughter of Twilight
Mothered of Midnight
Father of Daylight and Dawn;
Shadow of Sunlight
Shimmering Starlight,
Sister of Forest and Fawn!
Maid of a Morrow,
Mistress of Sorrow
Mingled of Mourning and Mirth;
Born of World Brotherhood,
Crowned of All Motherhood,
Beauty of Heaven and Earth!

                                        --Crisis Magazine

                    _____

The true worth of a race must be measured by the character of
its womanhood.

--Mary McLeod Bethune

———

When you dance
Do you thing of Spain,--
Purple skirts and clipping castanets,
Creole Girl?

When you laugh,
Do you think of France,--
Golden wine and mincing minuets,
Creole Girl?

When you sing
Do you think of young America,--
Grey guns and battling bayonets,
Creole Girl?

When you cry,
Do you think of Africa,--
Blue nights and casual canzonets,
Creole Girl?

--Leslie Morgan Collins

———

She does not know her beauty
She thinks her body
Has no glory

If she could dance
Naked
Under palm trees
And see her image in the river
She would know

But there are no palms
On the street
And dishwater gives back no images.

--Waring Cuney

———

The master subjected her to the most elemental form of
terrorism distinctly suited to the female: rape.

--Angela Davis

———

I shall forgive the white south much in its final judgment day: I shall forgive its slavery, for slavery is a world old habit; I shall forgive its fighting for a well-lost cause, and for remembering that struggle with tender tears; I shall forgive its so called "pride of race," the passion of its hot blood, and even its dear, old, laughable strutting and posing; but one thing I shall never forgive, neither in this world nor the world to come: its wanton and continued and persistent insulting of the black womanhood, which it sought and seeks to prostitute to its lust.

--W.E.B. Dubois

Black woman of beauty, thou has given color to the world.
Among other women thou art Royal and the fairest. . . .

--Marcus Garvey

Her body
  sways like
A yellow
  Calla Lilly
To the
  Wild music
of the wind.

--Opportunity Magazine

Were it mine to select a woman
 As queen of the hall of fame;
One who has fought the gamest fight
 And climbed down from the depths of shame;
I would have to give the sceptre
 To the lowliest of them;
She, who has struggled through the years,
 With her back against the wall
Wronged by the men of an alien race,
 Deserted by those of her own;
With a prayer in her heart, a song on her lips
 She carried the fight alone.

--Andrea Razafkeriefo

Naked woman, black woman
Dressed in your color which is life.
Naked woman, dark woman,
Firm fleshed ripe fruit,
somber ecstacies of black wine.

--Black Opheus
Senghor

It has been hard for black women to emerge from the myriad of
distorted images that have portrayed us as grinning Beulahs,
castrating Sapphires, and pancake-box Jemimahs.

--Margaret Sloan

* * *

BLESSING

Oh Lord have mercy upon us
And keep away some of our neighbors from us,
For every day they come down upon us
And eat all our victuals.

--Black Saying

* * *

BLIND

The only people who are really blind are those whose eyes are
so obscured by hatred and bigotry that they can't see the light of
love and justice.

--Stevie Wonder

* * *

BLUES

Woke up this morning feeling sad an blue
Woke up this morning feeling sad an blue
Didn't have nobody to tell my troubles to.

--Anglo African Magazine

———

Got the riverfront blues, baby and I'm blue as I can be.
Got the riverfront blues, baby and I'm blue as I can be.
That ole Mississippi sure is making a fool out of me.

--Black Saying

———

O hoarse-voiced lady, sing
the Georgia Blues.
And wring your hand, and
roll your bulging eyes;
Coil and uncoil yourself, and melodize.
Those tales of dark men who must love and bruise;
Oh Sing the Blues
Georgia Blues.

--Milton Brighte

———

I've got the St. Louis Blues, I am as blue as I can be.

--W.C. Handy

———

I got the weary Blues and I can't be satisfied.
Got the weary Blues and I can't be satisfied--
I ain't happy no mo
And I wish I had died.

--Langston Hughes

* * *

BOOKS

Many books written of persons and things have their beginnings and their ending in fancy, without special design for the elevation of mind or the culture of literary taste and pure morals, but for entertainment and amusement and gratification of sentiment without the reader in any sense in mind.

--M.A. Majors

* * *

BOURGEOISE

Since the black bourgeoise is composed chiefly of white-collar workers and since its small business enterprises are insignificant in the American economy, the black bourgeoise wields no political power as a class in American society.

--E. Franklin Frazier

* * *

BOY

Ol' John Lee was a terrible ol' man;
Raised hell all over the lan'
Cause there's one thing ol' John couldn't stan
Was to called boy instead of man.

--David Mac Adoo

* * *

BRAVERY

Brave actions never want a trumpet.

--Afro American

* * *

BROTHERHOOD

I believe in God, who made of one blood all nations that on earth do dwell. I believe that all men, black and brown and white, are brothers, varying through time and opportunity, in form and gift and feature, but differing in no essential particular, and alike in soul and the possibility of infinite development.

--W.E.B. Dubois

We had our share of differences with white soldiers when we were sitting around England, but since we have all been over here getting shot at together, we have been getting along fine.

--Sgt. Leo G. Edward

I want to be the white man's brother, not his brother-in-law.

--Martin Luther King Jr.

We must learn to live together as brothers or perish together as fools.

--Martin Luther King Jr.

We do not want the man of another color for our brothers-in-law, but we do want them for our brothers.

--Booker T. Washington

* * *

BURDEN

The burden that is placed on you because you're a Negro male is terrifying.

--James Baldwin

So for generations in the mind of America, the Negro has been more of a formula than a human being- a something to be argued about, condemned or defended, to be worried over, harassed or patronized, a social bodgey or a social burden.

--Alain Locke

* * *

BUSINESS

Despite the dreams of Negro leaders at the turn of the century that Negro businessmen would become organizers of big industries and large financial undertakings, Negroes have not become captains of industries nor even the managers of large corporations.

--E. Franklin Frazier

* * *

BUSY

A person has to be busy to be alive.

--Marion Anderson

C

CAPITALISM

A capitalistic system automatically includes racism, whether by design or not.

--Stokely Carmichael

_____

Capitalism and racism go hand in hand.

--Stokely Carmichael

*   *   *

CAUSE

We wish to plead our own cause. Too long have others spoken for us.

--Freedom's Journal
Samuel E. Cornish
John B. Russwurm

*   *   *

CAUTION

You better not shake hands wid a crawfish.

--Black Saying

* * *

CHANCE

Chance has never yet satisfied the hope of a suffering people. Action, self-reliance, the vision of self and the future have been the only means by which the oppressed have seen and realized the light of their own freedom.

--Marcus Garvey

* * *

CHANGE

Not everything that is faced can be changed at once, but nothing can be changed until it is faced.

--James Baldwin

No one is qualified to change the system he does not understand. Education brings that understanding.

--George E. Johnson

He who cannot change the very fabric of his thought will never be able to change reality, and will never therefore, be able to make progress.

--Anwar el-Sadat

* * *

CHARACTER

Wherever man goes to dwell, his character goes with him.

--African Proverb

* * *

CHARISMA

Charisma is a gift of the spirit.

--Jesse Jackson

* * *

CHILD

It is a bad child who does not take advice.

--African Proverb

The child hates him who gives it all it warts.

--African Proverb

The child that has never been into a strange town, says its mother cooks best.

--Afro American

Sometimes I feel like a motherless child
Sometimes I feel like a motherless child
A long way from home.

--Black Spiritual

* * *

CHILDREN

Children's talent to endure stems from their ignorance of alternatives.

--Maya Angelou

_____

All God's children play together in the streets of heaven.

--Black Maxim

_____

I expect that this generation of Negro children throughout the United States will grow up stronger and better because of the courage and dignity and suffering of the nine children of Little Rock and their counterparts in Nashville, Clinton and Sturges.

--Martin Luther King Jr.

_____

Riches and pride of life are naught but transitory, we are children of the same God, brothers on our journey.

--Armand Lanusse

_____

There are many things I think of, as my days come to a close.
Of all the things I may have been, why motherhood I chose.
I could have been a lawyer, a teacher or a nurse,
With these at least, I'd always have some money in my purse.

I could have had a fine large home, two cars and jewels of gold,
If I had taken time to travel down a different road.
I chose to fill my life with children, one every other year,
To hug, to kiss, to hold them and keep them safe from fear.

I may never have a large fine home, two cars or jewels of gold.
I have a heart that's full of love for every child I hold.
I've not only been a lawyer, a teacher and a nurse,
I've held every position that man made upon this earth.

I've heard great men make many speeches, as this world they try to
    steer,
But the greatest sound in all of life, is, "I love you mommy dear."
Of all the roads I could have chosen that's best and good.
Is the one that took me up the path to wonderful motherhood.

--Mary M. Tyler

_____

We must provide constructive activities for our children.

--Malcolm X

*   *   *

CHOICE

We can choose either to walk the high road of human brotherhood or to tread the low road of man's inhumanity to man. How we deal with this crucial situation will determine our moral health as individuals and our prestige as a leader of the free world. If America is to remain a first class nation, it cannot have a second class citizenship.

--Martin Luther King Jr.

*   *   *

CHRISTIAN

Lord, I want to be a Christian
In my heart, in-a my heart
Lord, I want to be a Christian
In my heart.

--Black Spiritual

The only Christian churches in the United States are those that welcome and encourage the participation of all the sons of man.

--Adam Clayton Powell Jr.

*   *   *

CHRISTIANITY

We have destroyed the wonder of Christianity and replaced it with the ordinariness of Church-anity.

--Adam Clayton Powell Jr.

*   *   *

CHURCH

The church, of course is the greatest force in the lives of our people.

--Etta Moten

As among our people generally the Church is the Alpha and Omega of all things.

--Martin Delany

*　*　*

CIRCUMSPECT

Behind every rolling ball there's a running boy.

--Unknown

*　*　*

CITIZENSHIP

We're citizens of two lands--Africa by heritage and here by investment.

--Jesse　Jackson

If I had to choose between baseball's Hall of Fame and first class citizenship for all of my people, I would say first-class citizenship.

--Jackie Robinson

*　*　*

CIVIL RIGHTS

I consider myself a beneficiary of the civil rights movement.

--Patricia Roberts Harris

I am a radical and I am going to stay one until my people get free to walk the earth. Negroes just cannot wait for civil rights. This year it's a ball player, next year we'll have a professional basketball player, and that's only the beginning.

--Paul Robeson

The Negro may wind up with a mouthful of civil rights, but an empty stomach and living in a hovel.

--Whitney M. Young Jr.

* * *

CLASS STRUGGLE

In the modern world today, in the era of neo-colonialism, the class struggle has become the race struggle. In other words, it is not only a class struggle, but racial too. Race forms the class struggle in the modern world.

--Kwame Nkrumah

* * *

COLONIALISM

Colonialism . . . is a violence in its natural state, and it will yield only when confronted with greater violence.

--Stokely Carmichael

* * *

COLOR

You can't tell a black man by the color of his skin.

--James Baldwin

Take away an accident of pigmentation of our outer skin and there is no difference between me and someone else.

--Shirley Chisholm

When people like me, they tell me it is in spite of my color. When they dislike me, they point out it is not because of my color.

--Frantz Fanon

* * *

COMFORT

It is small comfort to a mother who stays awake all night in a hovel, keeping rats away from her child to tell her that in another generation things are going to get better.

--Whitney Young Jr.

* * *

COMMONALITY

The question is: can the white and colored people of this country be blended into a common nationality, and enjoy together, in the same country, under the same flag, the inestimable blessings of life, liberty, and the pursuit of happiness, as neighborly citizens of a common country? I answer most unhesitantly, I believe they can.

--Frederick Douglass

* * *

COMMUNISM

Grass roots Blacks are not so skeptical of communism. It's your middle class Blacks who have the most hostility.

--Angela Davis

_____

Negroes must continue to realize that communism is no solution to their problems.

--Thurgood Marshall

* * *

COMMUNISTS

There are as many communists in the freedom movement as there are eskimos in Florida.

--Martin Luther King Jr.

* * *

COMMUNITY

Black people got to act as a black community, and the Democratic and Republican Parties are completely irrelevant to them.

--Adam Clayton Powell Jr.

* * *

COMPANION

A wicked companion invites us all to hell.

--African Proverb

* * *

COMPANY

Go not to hell for company.

          --Afro American

* * *

CONCOMITANT

When the occasion comes, the proverb comes.

          --African Proverb

* * *

CONDUCT

We need a real challenge to corporate conduct.

          --Jesse Jackson

* * *

CONGRESS

The mechanism of legislation in the United States Congress is a wondrous labyrinth of frustration.

          --Adam Clayton Powell Jr.

———

I don't want to have any more than any other Congressman. But by the grace of God I'm not going to take any less.

          --Adam Clayton Powell Jr.

* * *

CONSCIENCE

A clear conscience is a good pillow.

--African Proverb

* * *

CONSCIOUSNESS

The white man cannot give Negroes black consciousness. They have to give it to each other.

--Alvin Poussaint

* * *

CONTENTMENT

A contented man is always rich.

--African Proverb

I will not be content until a black man can make everything he uses, from a pair of shoes to an airplane.

--Leon H. Sullivan

* * *

CONTEST

Remember that in a contest with oppression, the almighty has no attribute which can take sides with oppressors.

--Frederick Douglass

* * *

COURAGE

Boasting is not courage.

--African Proverb

_____

And somehow it was borne upon my brain
How being dark, and living through the pain of it, is courage more
than angels have.

--Countee Cullen

*   *   *

CREATION

The western world has created me, given me my name; has hidden
my truth as a permanent and historical fact. I may recover from
this and I may not. I'm a grim man, old and insane enough to tell
you that not many survive being born black in America.

--James Baldwin

*   *   *

CREED

We want freedom. We want power to determine the destiny of
our Black Community.

--Black Panthers

*   *   *

CRIME

The world has made being a black a crime. . . . I hope to make
it a virtue.

--Marcus Garvey

*   *   *

CRITICISM

Do not tell the man who is carrying you that he stinks.

--African Proverb

*   *   *

CROWD

A bed for two isn't a bed for three.

--Creole Slave Proverb

*   *   *

CRUCIFIXION

Were you there when they crucified my Lord?
Oh, sometimes it causes me to tremble.

--Black Spiritual

*   *   *

CRY

Hushaby, don't you cry,
Go to sleepy, little baby.
When you wake, you shall have cake, and all the pretty little
  horses.
Blacks and bays, dapples and grays,
Coach and six-a little horses.

Way down yonder in the meadow,
There's a poor little lambie;
The bees and the butterflies picking out his eyes,
The poor little thing cries
                    Mammy

Hushaby, don't you cry
Go to sleepy, little baby.

--Black Slave Saying

*   *   *

CULTURE

There is a mistaken idea that culture means to paint a little,
sing a little, dance a little, put on haughty airs, and to quote
passages from popular books. It means nothing of the kind.
Culture means politeness, charity, fairness, good temper and good
conduct. Culture is not a thing to make a display of.

--Colored American

First, we come from Africa. We had to learn English. We had,
in other words, to create ourselves as a people--and this I take
right down to the racial, the bloodlines, the mingling of African
blood with bloodlines indigenous to the New World. A few people
can trace their connections back to a given African tribe, but for
most of us, no. We can't even trace our blood back to Africa
because most of us are part Indian, Spanish, Irish, part any and
every damn thing. But culturally, we represent a synthesis of a
number of elements. And that's a problem of abstraction in itself.

--Ralph Ellison

The American Negro is neither totally African nor totally
Western. He is Afro-American, a true hybrid, a combination of two
cultures.

--Martin Luther King Jr.

The irony of the situation is that in folk-lore, folk-song,
folk-dance and popular music the things recognized as
characteristically and uniquely American are products of the
despised slave minority. . . . What accounts for it in the past
and promises great momentum to it in the future is the simple fact
that of the intensification of the emotional side of life by
persecution and suffering. . . . This is the Negro's compensation
for his hard lot and generation long sacrifice.

--Alain Locke

One of the great measures of a people is its culture, its
artistic stature.

--Paul Robeson

*   *   *

CURIOSITY

Curiosity often leads men into bitterness.

--African Proverb

D

DANCE

He who cannot dance will say: 'The drum is bad'

--African Proverb

————

We must never forget that the dance is the cradle of Negro music.

--Alain Locke

————

The Negro has more records than books and is dancing his life away.

--Ron Krenga

*   *   *

DAY

The longest day is sure to have its night.

--Afro American

————

The worst of some days is the best of others.

--African Proverb

*   *   *

DEATH

Death does not sound a trumpet.

--African Proverb

Fear is no obstacle to death.

--African Proverb

All death is sudden to the unprepared.

--Afro American

Six feet of earth makes all men equal.

Afro American

Death has no respect for color.

--Black Maxim

The quicker death, the quicker heaven.

--Black Maxim

The death train is always on time.

--Black Maxim

It's when death comes that you think about your life.

--Creole Slave Proverb

Dead men are wisest, for they know
How far the roots of flowers go,
How long a seed must rot to grow.

--Countee Cullen

If I die, it will be for a good cause.

--Medgar Evers

I hope when I am dead that I shall lie
In some deserted grave- I cannot tell you why,
But I should like to sleep in some neglected spot,
Unknown to every one, by everyone forgot.

--Jessie Fauset

He who lives not uprightly, dies completely in the crumbling
of the physical body, but he who lives well, transforms himself
from that which is mortal, to immortal.

--Marcus Garvey

It is better to die than to grow up and find that you are
colored.

--Fenton Johnson

When I die my song shall be the crooning of the summer breeze.

--Fenton Johnson

Every second of our lives is devoted to battling against death.

--Jack Johnson

If we must die- let it not be like hogs.

--Claude McKay

All the thirst for pure affection,
  All the hunger of the heart;
All the vain amid tearful cryings,
  All forever now depart.

Clasp the pale and faded fingers,
  O'er the cold and lifeless form;
They shall never shrink and shiver,
  Homeless in the dark and storm.

Press the death-weights calmly, gently,
  O'er the eyelids in their sleep;
Tears shall never tremble from them,
  They shall never wake to weep.

Close the silent lips together,
  Lips once parted with a sign;
Through their sealed, moveless portals,
  N'er shall float a bitter cry.

                    --Frances Ellen Watkins

                *   *   *

DEBT

   America owes my people some of the dividends. I shall make
them understand that there is a debt to the Negro people which
they never can repay.

                    --Sojourner Truth

                *   *   *

DECISION

   In every decision I made, in every action I took, I have been
directed by my firm belief in the dignity of man and his right to
freedom, to peace, and to equality.

                    --Anwar el-Sadat

                *   *   *

DEEDS

A man's deeds are his life.

Afro American

_____

Good deeds remain, all things else perish.

--Afro American

* * *

DEMOCRACY

I swear to the Lord
I still can't see
Why Democracy means
Everybody but me.

--Langston Hughes

* * *

DEPARTURES

Hit the road Jack and don't look back.

--Black Maxim

* * *

DEPRESSION

A fishing pole and garden patch is the best way to survive a depression.

--Black Maxim

* * *

DESERTION

It sometimes seems we are deserted by earth and heaven.

--Frederick Douglass

* * *

DESIRE

I've lived to bury my desires,
And see my dreams corrode with rust;
Now all that's left is fruitless fires
That burn my empty heart to dust.

--Alexander Pushkin

* * *

DESTINY

Abused and scorned though we may be, our destiny is tied up with the destiny of America.

--Martin Luther King Jr.

And my father and mother strengthened me in this my first impression, saying in my presence, I was intended for some great purpose.

--Nat Turner

* * *

DEVELOPMENT

The development of human society- from tribalism to feudalism, to capitalism, to socialism- is brought about by the needs and aspirations of mankind for a better life.

--Paul Robeson

* * *

DEVIL

The devil seeks to destroy all that we love.

--Black Maxim

_____

If you want to see the devil fall
Hit him with the Gospel ball,
But the devil wears an iron shoe,
And if you don't watch it,
He will put it on you.

--Black Saying

_____

In every ruin we find a devil.

--Afro American

_____

The devil never gives up!

--Black Maxim

_____

When it is raining and the sun is shining, the devil is
beating his wife.

--Black Folklore

_____

If you ask the devil to dinner it will be hard to get him out
of the house again.

--Creole Slave Proverb

_____

I believe in the Devil and his angels, who wantonly work to
narrow the opportunity of struggling human beings, especially if
they be black.

--W.E.B. Dubois

_____

Do you wish to renounce the Devil?
Asked a good priest of a woman of evil
Who had so many sins that every year
They cost her endless remorse and fear.
"I wish to renounce him forever," she said,
"But that I may lose every urge to be bad,
Before pure grace takes me in hand
Shouldn't I show my daughter how to get a man?"

--Armand Lanusse

    The devil is mad and I am glad, he lost the soul he thought he had.

--Slave Spiritual

*   *   *

DEVILMENT

A brown skin woman went walkin' down Rampart Street
Got devilment in her eyes
That walk she got make you think
She's got devilment in her thighs.

--Black Saying

*   *   *

DIED

Wish I'd died when I was a baby,
O 'Lord rock a jubilee,
Wish I'd died

--Slave Song

*   *   *

DIGNITY

The most luxurious possession, the richest treasure anybody has, is his personal dignity.

--Jackie Robinson

* * *

DISCRIMINATION

Despite professions of equality, America and Americans exercise racial discrimination against millions of dark American citizens practically from the day of their birth.

--Daisy Bates

* * *

DREAM

In the days of my youth not a dream had I, good Lord!
These times I am growing old, full of dreams am I good Lord!
I have dreams of those good times gone by!

--Creole Slave Song

Good morning daddy!
Ain't you heard
The boogie-woogie rumble of a dream deferred?

--Langston Hughes
Dream Boogie

What happens to a dream deferred?

--Langston Hughes

I have a dream that my four little children will one day live
in a nation where they will not be judged by the color of their
skin but by the content of their character.

When we let freedom ring, when we let it ring from every
village and every hamlet, from every state and every city, we will
be able to speed up that day when all of God's children, black men
and white men, Jews and Gentiles, Protestants and Catholics, will
be able to join hands and sing, in the words of the old Negro
Spiritual.

Free at last
Free at last
Thank God Almighty
We are free at last.

--Martin Luther King Jr.

* * *

DRUM

For I am my mother's daughter and the drums of Africa still
beat in my heart. They will not let me rest while there is a
single Negro boy or girl without a chance to prove his worth.

--Mary McLeod Bethune

* * *

E

ECONOMY

The Negro works on a two fold economy. He buys what he wants and begs what he needs.

--Ron Karenga

*   *   *

EDUCATION

I am convinced that the real solution is education.

--Marva Collins

_____

A good education is something no one can ever take away from you.

--Black Maxim

*   *   *

EMOTION

His immense emotional capacity is the Negro's great asset.

--Paul Robeson

*   *   *

END

There can be only one end, one decision in this fight- and that will be a knockout for the axis.

--Joe Louis

*   *   *

ENDS

The ends you serve that are selfish will take you no further than yourself, but the ends you serve that are for all, in common, will take you even into eternity.

--Marcus Garvey

*   *   *

ENEMY

An intelligent enemy is better than a stupid friend.

--African Proverb

*   *   *

ENGLISH

The fact is that there is an appalling amount of ignorance amongst English people regarding the Negro and his doing.

--Samuel Coleridge Taylor

*   *   *

EQUAL

Personally, I consider myself the equal of any white man who ever lived, and no one could ever change me in that respect.

--Samual Coleridge Taylor

*   *   *

EQUALITY

Real equality, even in the United States of America, will be impossible if the white race is to be a race of owners and managers, and the Negro-race is to be a race of employees.

--Edward Brooke

_____

Thomas Jefferson wrote in the Declaration of Independent of the equality of man, but he did not mean us. Jefferson and George Washington both died without freeing their slaves.

--Benjamin E. Mays

_____

I'm goin' to eat at the welcome table,
O yes I'm goin' to eat at the welcome table some of these days
    hallelujah!

--Black Spiritual

_____

Black is white and white is black.

--Walter White

*   *   *

EULOGY

If any of you are around when I have to meet my day, I don't want a long funeral. And if you get somebody to delivery the eulogy, tell them not to talk too long. Every now and then I wonder what I want them to say. Tell them not to mention that I have a Nobel Prize, that isn't important. Tell them not to mention that I have three or four hundred other awards, that's not important. Tell them not to mention where I went to school.
I'd like somebody to mention that day, that . . . "Martin Luther King, Jr., tried to give his life serving others." I'd like for somebody to say that day, that . . . "Martin Luther King Jr., tried to love somebody." I want you to say that day, that . . . "I tried to be right on the war question." I want you to be able to say that day, that . . . "I did try to feed the hungry." And I want you to be able to say that day, that . . . "I did try, in my life, to clothe those who were naked." I want you to say on that day, that . . . "I did try, in my life, to visit those who were in prison." I want you to say that . . . "I tried to love humanity."

                                        --Martin Luther King, Jr.

                    *   *   *

EVIL

Evil enters like a needle and spreads like an oak tree.

                                        --African Proverb

Evil knows where evil sleeps.

                                        --African Proverb

                    *   *   *

EXIGENCY

When the snake is in the house, one need not discuss the matter at length.

--African Proverb

*   *   *

EXPECTATION

The Black man in America is playing against a loaded deck, but still is expected to win.

--James Wilson

*   *   *

F

FACISM

The Negro is a born anti-facist.

--Adam Clayton Powell Jr.

*   *   *

FAILURE

To try and fail is not laziness.

--African Proverb

*   *   *

FALSEHOOD

The path of falsehood has seven endings.

--African Proverb

One falsehood spoils a thousand truths.

--African Proverb

* * *

FATE

Fate made me a boxer.

--Jack Johnson

* * *

FEAR

A scared Negro is one thing. A mad Negro is something else.

--Dick Gregory

How deadly an enemy is fear!
How it seeks out the areas of our vulnerability and savages us
Until we are so rent and battered and desperate
that we resort to what revolts us and wallow in the foulest
  treachery
One wishes for death with a kind of defiant defeatism
Wishing that the worst may befall since the nearly-worst has so
  often befallen:
it is not a wish for oblivion but a pugnacious assertion of
  discontent
A disgust at the boundless opprobrium of life
a desperation; despair

--Dennis Brutus

* * *

FEIGN

All who snore are not asleep.

--Afro American

*   *   *

FEMININE MYSTIQUE

The wiles of woman (which are known to men) are ninety-and-nine, but not even satan has discovered the hundredth.

--Afro American

*   *   *

FIDELITY

When your hen is laying, don't put her in the pot.

--Creole Prove

FILM

I thought I could do something for the Negro race in the films; showthe truth about them- and about other people too. I used to do my part and go away feeling satisfied. Thought everything was okay, well it wasn't. Things were twisted and changed-distorted. They didn't mean the same. That made me think things out. It made me more conscious politically.

--Paul Robeson

*   *   *

FOOL

A fool and water will go the way they are diverted.

--African Proverb

_____

When a fool is told a proverb, its meaning has to be explained to him.

--African Proverb

_____

By the time the fool has learned the game, the players have dispersed.

--African Proverb

_____

When a fool is being cursed, he thinks he is being praised.

--African Proverb

_____

Old fools have forgotten more than young fools know.

--African Proverb

_____

There is nothing worse than an educated fool

--Black Maxim

_____

Dogs make their dinner upon what belongs to fools.

--Creole Proverb

_____

A fool always finds a greater fool that admires him.

--African Proverb

* * *

FORCE

A little subtleness is better than a lot of force.

                                        --African Proverb

                    *   *   *

FORTITUDE

It takes fortitude to be a man and no less to be an artist.

                                        --Ralph Ellison
                    _____

Up you mighty race, you can accomplish what you will.

                                        --Marcus Garvey

                    *   *   *

FORTUNE

Fortune is not far from the brave man's head.

                                        --Afro American

                    *   *   *

FREEDOM

I was very young when I first went to Europe. I was 18 years
old. But I had to go. I wanted to find freedom. I couldn't find
it in St. Louis.

                                        --Josephine Baker
                    _____

Mr. Lincoln had told our race we were free, but mentally we were still enslaved.

--Mary Mcleod Bethune

_____

Freedom resides within the soul.

--Black Maxim

_____

No people can be free who themselves do not constitute an essential part of the ruling element of the country in which they live.

--Martin Delany

_____

Those who profess to favor freedom and yet depreciate agitation are those who want crops without plowing up the ground-they want rain without thunder and lightening.

--Frederick Douglass

_____

If freedom is good for any, it is good for all.

--Prince Hall

_____

There is no price in the world too great to pay for freedom.

--Martin Luther King Jr.

_____

The essence of man is found in freedom.

--Martin Luther King Jr.

_____

We believe Black people will not be free until we are able to determine our destiny.

--Black Panthers

_____

Our white allies know that they cannot be free while we are
not.

--A. Phillip Randolph

Salvation for a race, nation, or class must come from within.
Freedom is never granted; it is won.

--A. Phillip Randolph

We shall, we will, be free men.

--Roy Wilkins

The American Negro has changed his temper. Now he wants his
freedom. Whether he is smiling at you or not, he wants his
freedom. The old exploitation of peoples is definitely past.

--Paul Robeson

Mammy, don't you cook no more,
You are free, you are free!
Rooster, don't you crow no more,
You are free, you are free!
Old hen, don't you lay no more eggs,
You are free, you free!

--Slave Saying

Go down Moses
'Way down in Egypt land,
Tell ole Pharoah,
To let my people go.

--Black Spiritual

Nobody can give you freedom.

--Malcolm X

*   *   *

FREE ENTERPRISE

The free enterprise system is still very much a myth for black folks in America.

--Dick Gregory

* * *

FREE THOUGHT

If a free thought seek expression, Speak it boldly- speak it all.

--Martin Delany

* * *

FRIEND

A close friend can become a close enemy.

--African Proverb

* * *

FRIENDS

To be without a friend, is to be poor, indeed.

--African Proverb

* * *

FUNERAL

At the funeral of a rich man you find tears in the eyes and keys in the hands.

--African Proverb

* * *

G

GENEALOGY

The reader must not expect me to say much of my family.
Genealogical trees do not flourish among slaves.

--Frederick Douglass

*   *   *

GENTLEMAN

A true gentleman will respect woman even in her weakness.

--Afro American

*   *   *

GOALS

The sweetest of grapes hang highest.

--Afro American

*   *   *

<u>GOD</u>

God delays, but does not forget.

--Afro American

_____

If the concept of God has any validity or use, it can only be to make it larger, freer and more loving. If God cannot do this, it is tme we got rid of him.

--James Baldwin

_____

God has been replaced, as he has all over the west, with respectability and air conditioning.

--Amamu Baraka

_____

One with God is a majority.

--Frederick Douglass

_____

I believe in God who made of one blood all races that dwell on earth.

--W.E.B. Dubois

_____

My mother started telling me about God when I was very young. There was never any talk about red people, brown people, black people, or yellow people, or about the differences that existed between them. I don't remember exactly when, but I was quite grown when I first heard about all that. I am sure my mother felt that God took some rich black soil, some red clay, and some white sand, and mixed them all together to make the first man, so that forever after no man would feel he was better than another.

--Duke Ellington

_____

I never grope for methods; the method is revealed at the moment I am inspired to create something new. Without God to draw aside the curtain, I would be helpless.

--George Washington Carver

_____

So be wise and satisfied with the joy that comes to you
through the reflection and miracle of God, such as all the wonders
and beauty we live with and are exposed to on earth.

--Duke Ellington

Well thank God there is a God, that will neutralize Hitler and
neutralize neutron bombs.

Dick Gregory

Take away the highest ideal--Faith and Confidence In A
God--and mankind at large is reduced to savagery and the race
destroyed.

--Marcus Garvey.

We are all endowed with the same universal God-force.

--Dick Gregory

What is God?
All the beauty and truth and goodness in the world!

--Adam Clayton Powell Jr.

Without the hand of God in man's hand, there can be no coming
together of black and white in this world.

--Adam Clayton Powell Jr.

* * *

GOOD

The good thing sells itself.

--African Proverb

Good still has a way of growing out of evil. The blood of these girls must serve as a revitalizing force to bring light to this dark city.

> Martin Luther King Jr.
> Tribute To Black girls
> Killed In Bombing of
> Black Church In Birmingham

* * *

GOSSIP

Gossiping and lying go together.

> --Afro American

* * *

GRATITUDE

Gratitude is the least of virtues; ingratitude the worst of vices.

> --Afro American

* * *

GRAVEYARD

O graveyard, O graveyard,
I'am walking troo de graveyard;
Lay dis body down.

> --Black Spiritual

GREATNESS

A great man does not like to be obscured by surroundings.

--African Proverb

_____

From great rivers come great fish.

--Afro American

_____

From small beginnings come great things.

--Afro American

_____

A nation's greatness is not dependent upon the things it makes and uses.

--Anna J. Cooper

_____

Each generation has its own call to greatness.

--Jesse Jackson

_____

Vice alone is low, virtue holds ranks;
The greatest man is he who is most just.

--Armand Lanusse

*   *   *

GREED

You want all, you lose all.

--African Proverb

*   *   *

GREENS

Don't you love em
Don't you love em
Greasy greens, Lawd, Greasy greens.

--Harlem Street Sellers Cry

* * *

GRIEF

Grief pent up will burst the heart.

--Afro American
_____

No day passes without some grief.

--Afro American

* * *

H

HANGING

Alas! young men, come, make lament
For Poor St. Malo in distress!
They chased, they hunted him with dogs
They fired at him with a gun.

They hauled him from the cypress swamps
His arms they tied behind his back,
They tied his hands in front of him;
They tied him to a horses tail,
They dragged him up into the town.

Before those grand Cabildo men
They charged that he had made a plot
To cut the throats of all the whites.
They asked him who his comrades were;

Poor St. Malo said not a word!
The judge his sentence read to him,
And they raised the gallows tree.
They drew the horse--the cart moved off- and left St. Malo
  hanging there.
The sun was up an hour high
When on the levee he was hung
They left the body swinging there.
For carrion crows to feed upon.

--Century Magazine

*   *   *

HAPPINESS

I believe that no man can be happy within himself if he ever surrenders his dignity and self respect.

--Ralph Bunche

Happiness lives nowhere,
Some old fool said,
If not within oneself

--Langston Hughes

*   *   *

HARLEM

New York isn't New York if you're a Negro--it's Harlem.

--James Baldwin

Ah, heart of me, the weary, weary feet.
In Harlem wandering from street to street.

--Claude McKay

*   *   *

HATE

The price of hating other human beings is loving oneself less.

--Eldridge Cleaver

I imagine one of the reasons people cling to their hates so stubbornly is because they sense, once hate is gone, they will be forced to deal with pain.

--James Baldwin

I never learned to hate at home, or shame. I had to go to school for that.

>   --Dick Gregory

Hate cannot drive out hate: only love can do that.

>   --Martin Luther King Jr.

My husband never hated. He never despaired of well being.

>   --Coretta Scott King

Hate is just as injurious to the hater as it is to the hated.

>   --Martin Luther King Jr.

Many of our inner conflicts are rooted in hate.

>   --Martin Luther King Jr.

I don't hate nobody for what they did to me.

>   --Clarence Norris
>   Scottsboro Boy

*   *   *

HATRED

There is no medicine to cure hatred.

>   --African Proverb

*   *   *

HEAD

Use your head for more than a hat rack.

--Black Maxim

* * *

HEALTH

Men know how to build up and maintain big fortunes, but they do not know how to maintain their health--the greatest fortune of all.

--Jack Johnson

* * *

HEART

The heart of a fool is in his mouth and the mouth of the wise man is in his heart.

--African Proverb

* * *

HEAVEN

I know de udder worl' is not Like Dis.

--Black Spiritual

_____

Heaven must be better than this!

--Slave Saying

_____

When we all meet in heaven,
There is no parting there;
When we all meet in heaven,
There is no parting no more.

--Jacob Stroyer

* * *

HELL

In hell there are no fans.

--African Proverb

———

When I was coming along, a black man had hell.

--Louis Armstrong

———

If hell is what we are taught it is, then there will be more
christians there than in all creation.

--Marcus Garvey

* * *

HERITAGE

We are the descendants of slaves. We are the offsprings of
noble men and women who were kidnapped from their native land and
chained in ships like beasts. We are the heirs of a great and
exploited continent known as Africa.

--Martin Luther King Jr.

* * *

HEROES

We think the people are the heroes of life.

--Huey Newton

* * *

HIDE

He can run but he can't hide.

--Joe Louis
  Description of Opponent Billy Conn

* * *

HIDING

If you are in hiding, don't light a fire.

--African Proverb

* * *

HINDSIGHT

Look back, I entreat you.

--Benjamin Banneka

* * *

HISTORY

No matter where you travel
You still be black
You carry all your history,
On your own damn back.

--Houston Baker

———

History is the land-mark by which we are directed into the
true course of life. The history of a movement, the history of a
nation, the history of a race is the guide post of that movement's
destiny, that nation's destiny, that race's destiny.

--Marcus Garvey

———

We are creatures of history, for every historical epoch has
its roots in a preceding epoch.

--A. Phillip Randolph

———

History must restore what slavery took away, for it is the
social damage of slavery that the present generation must repair
and offset.

--Arthur Schomburg

———

The amazing thing that history will record will be the fact
that most black people have for so long been so patient and have
retained a faith and confidence in a system that didn't deserve
it, and a system that now, not to prove to black people, but to
prove to its own young people, must change.

--Whitney M. Young, Jr.

*   *   *

HOLLYWOOD

Hollywood's not looking for my type. Dis, dat, dese- I can
learn to talk that way but not very well.

--Todd Duncan

*   *   *

HOME

The home is the foundation of a country's welfare.

--Jack Johnson

Home is where the gumbo is!

--Black Saying

This world is not my home
This world is not my home
This world is a howling wilderness,
This world is not my home.

--Black Spiritual

I look over Jordan, What did I see
   Coming for to carry me home?
A Golden Chariot, coming after me,
   Coming for to carry me home
Swing low, sweet chariot,
   Coming for to carry me home.

--Black Spiritual

* * *

HONESTY

No man can be honest with others unless he is true to himself.

--Anwar el-Sadat

* * *

HONOR

Honor withdraws from those who lie.

--Creole Slave Proverb

* * *

HOPE

Hope is the pillar of the world

--African Proverb

_____

Hope is the poor man's bread.

--Afro American

_____

Hope is the foundation of Black people's perseverance.

--Black Maxim

*   *   *

HUMAN JUDGMENT

To measure any man or to accept or reject him as a friend by any other standard than his individual worth is to deny oneself the vast benefits which come from knowing fellow human beings.

--Walter White

*   *   *

HUNGER

The hungry man does not hear.

--African Proverb

_____

When the bowels growl a fine coat won't make them hold their peace.

--Creole Slave Proverb

_____

The belly has no ears.

--Creole Slave Proverb

_____

Hungry men have no respect for law, authority or human life.

--Marcus Garvey

*　*　*

HURT

There is nothing that hurts like shame.

--African Proverb

*　*　*

My husband often told the children that if a man had nothing that was worth dying for, then he was not fit to live.

--Coretta Scott King

*　*　*

HYPOCRISY

One may smile and smile, and be a villian still.

--Afro American

*　*　*

I

IDEA

If you want to get across an idea, wrap it up in a person.

--Ralph Bunche

* * *

IDENTIFY

We tried to identify with white people so much that we refused
to admit that we had anything to do with Africa.

--Stokely Carmichael

* * *

IDLENESS

By doing nothing we learn to do evil.

--Afro American

Idleness is the rust of the soul.

--Afro American

* * *

IGNORANCE

Not to know is bad, not to wish to know is worse.

--African Proverb

* * *

ILLUSION

Not everything that has sugar is sweet.

--Creole Proverb

* * *

IMITATION

What the child says, he has heard at home.

--African Proverb

Copying everybody else all the time, the monkey one day cut his throat.

--African Proverb

Imitation runs deep in the black community in this country. It runs deep. You know, when we first got people to go to college and they went to the first white university in this country, there were things called fraternities and sororities. Our brothers and sisters could not get into these fraternities. They were kept out because of the color of their skin. So what did our brothers do? They turned around and formed something called Alphas, and only light-skinned Negroes could get in. Our black sisters, not to be outdone, formed AKA, for blue bloods only. The other dark-skinned

brothers, not to be outdone, set up Omega and Kappa. And then, of
course, we had the counterparts, the Deltas. Now wouldn't it have
been better if those people, instead of imitating a society that
had been built on excluding them, had turned around and built a
fraternity that included everybody, light skinned blacks and dark
skinned blacks. Perhaps that is the greatest problem you, as
black students face; you are never asked to create, only to
imitate.

--Stokely Carmichael

* * *

IMPATIENCE

The blackman in this country has been sitting on the hot stove
for nearly 400 years. And no matter how fast the brainwashers and
the brainwashed think they are helping him advance, it's still too
slow for the man whose behind is burning, on that hot stove.

--Malcolm X

* * *

IMPERFECTION

The brightest of all things the sun, has its spots.

--Afro American

* * *

INCITEMENT

Don't stir up dry manure.

--Creole Slave Proverb

* * *

INDEPENDENCE

I am not beside any finger says the thumb.

--African Proverb

———

I'm amazed when I pick up the paper and read that "England today decided to give independence to the West Indies." The whole west feels it has the right to give everybody their independence.
All men are born free, they are enslaved by other men; so the only act that the men who enslaved them can do is, not give them their independence, but stop oppressing them.

--Stokely Carmichael

———

I am unbossed and unbought.

--Shirley Chisholm

———

It's easy to be independent when you've got money. But to be independent when you haven't got a thing- that's the Lord's test.

--Mahalia Jackson

*   *   *

INDUSTRY

Industry is the parent of fortune.

--Afro American

*   *   *

INFERIORITY

The entire history of the Negro in the United States has been of a nature to create in the Negro a feeling of racial inferiority.

--E. Franklin Frazier

———

Racial tolerance and political equality of status have taken the place of oppression and slavery for the greater part of the negro race. But the suffering he has undergone has left an indeliable mark on the negro's soul, and at the present stage he suffers from an inferiority complex which finds its compenstaion in a desire to imitate the white man and his ways; but I am convinced that in this direction there is neither fulfillment nor peace for the negro.

--Paul Robeson

* * *

INFIDELITY

Too many cooks spoil the soup.

--Black Maxim

* * *

INFLATION

What is inflated too much, will burst into fragments.

--African Proverb

* * *

INGRATITUDE

Don't be ungrateful for another favor may be needed.

--Creole Slave Proverb

* * *

INITIATIVE

The first condition of being worthy of help from others is for an individual, race, or nation to do something for itself.

--A. Phllip Randolph

You can't just sit back and expect people to do things for you. You've got to get up and do it yourself.

--Diana Ross

* * *

INSTITUTIONS

The best defense of free American institutions is the heart of the American people themselves.

--Frederick Douglass

* * *

INSULT

Don't insult an alligator until after you've crossed the river.

--African Proverb

* * *

INSURRECTION

I have nothing more to offer than what George Washington would have had to offer had he been taken by the British and put to trial by them. I have adventured my life in endeavoring to obtain the liberty of my countrymen, and am a willing sacrifice to their cause.

Courtroom Testimony
Anonymous Black Insurrectionist 1804

* * *

INTEGRATING

The white man's "integrating" with black women has already changed the complexion and characteristics of the black race in America.

--Malcolm X

* * *

INTEGRATION

Integration means the man who 'makes it' leaving his black brothers behind in the ghetto as fast as his new sports car will take him.

--Stokely Carmichael

The word integration was invented by a Northern liberal.

--Malcolm X

* * *

INTELLECT

Developing intellectual power provides a key to understanding a hostile world, a key for coping with and ending injustices, and most important, the key to economic and political power. . . .

--Clifton R Wharton

* * *

INTERFERENCE

The goat's business is not the sheep's affair.

--Creole Proverb

* * *

INTERMARRIAGE

You're worried about me marrying your wife's daughter. I've been marrying your daughter ever since the days of slavery.

                                                    --James Baldwin

                        *   *   *

ISLAM

America needs to understand Islam, because this is the one religion that erases from its society the race problem.

                                                    --Malcolm X

                        *   *   *

J

JAZZ

In a Harlem cabaret
Six long-headed jazzers play.
A dancing girl who eyes are bold
Lifts high a dress of silkin gold.

--Langston Hughes

*   *   *

JESUS

Jesus keep me near the cross.

--Black Spiritual

*   *   *

JEWELS

Three jewels have I in my crown
Three gems beyond compare.
More precious they, tho less renown
Than any ruler wears.
Each has a heart of purest gold

Inset with love so true
That all are dazzled who behold
These gems of warm bright hue.
I keep them safe within my home.
Lest robbers steal my joy.
And never from my heart they roam
My wife, my girl and boy.

--J.H. Jones

*   *   *

JIM CROW

Where is the Jim Crow section
On this merry-go-round,
Mister, cause I want to ride?
Down South where I come from
White and colored
Can't sit side by side.

--Langston Hughes

*   *   *

JOGGING

We are all jogging,
Jogg, jog, jogging
And we're all jogging,
We are going

--Martin R. Delaney

*   *   *

JUDGMENT

'Tis the judgment of God that men reap The tares in madness they
sow.

--Frances E. W. Harper

*   *   *

JULY 4TH

I am not included within the pale of this glorious anniversary.

--Frederick Douglass

*   *   *

JUSTICE

Who is Justice? I would like to know,
Whom so ever she is, I would love her so.
I could love her, though my race
So seldom looks upon
        Love

--John Henrik Clarke

_____

We want justice for the so-called Negroes regardless of the price.

--Elijah Muhammad

*   *   *

K

KNOWLEDGE

Knowledge is better than riches.

--African Proverb

*   *   *

L

LABOR

The labourer is always in the sun; the landowner is always in
the shade.

--African Proverb

*   *   *

LAST

Tell me, Alexander, on your soul and conscience, do you
believe that anything of mine will last.

--Alexander Dumas pére

*   *   *

LAUGHTER

If I laugh loud enough, maybe no one will hear me cry.

--Velma McCloud

*   *   *

LAW

Lawmakers--law breakers

--African Proverb

_____

Law officers found a bullet hole above his right ear. The
left side of his face was crushed to the bone.

Description of Body of Emmitt Teal
Murdered for Whistling at a White Woman

_____

Any law that degrades human personality is unjust.

--Martin Luther King Jr.

_____

If our government cannot enforce the law in the south, it
should cease trying to enforce it all over the world.

--Thurgood Marshall

*   *   *

LEADERS

Chloroform your "Uncle Toms." The Negro must unload the
leeches and parasitic leaders who are absolutely eating the life
out of the struggling, deserving mass of people.

--Nannie Burroughs

_____

Real leaders are not appointed. Real leaders are not
elected. They lead in spite of elections and appointment, "they
come upon us."

--Spokesman Magazine

_____

It is not the time to follow in the path of white leaders; it
is time to be leaders ourselves

--New Orleans Tribune

*   *   *

LESSON

The lesson to black people, to my children, to everybody is
that you should always fight for your rights, even if it cost you
your life. Stand up for your rights, even if it kills you.
That's all that life consists of.

Clarence Norris
The Last of the Scottsboro Boys

*   *   *

LIBERAL

What the liberal really wants is to bring about change which
will not in any way endanger his position.

--Stokely Carmichael

*   *   *

LIBERTY

I believe in Liberty for all men; the space to stretch their
souls, the right to breathe and the right to vote, the freedom to
choose their friends, enjoy the sunshine and ride on the
railroads, uncursed by color; thinking, dreaming, working as they
will in a kingdom of beauty and love.

--W.E.B. Dubois

Liberty is a spirit sent out from God, and like its great
Author, is no respecter of persons.

--Henry Highland Garnet

*   *   *

LIE

My mother always taught me never to tell a lie unless you had rehearsed it with yourself first. She said if it didn't sound good to you, then you couldn't expect anybody to believe it.

--Satchel Paige

* * *

LIES

We have to understand the lies this country has spoken about black people and we have to set the record straight. No one else can do that but black people.

--Stokely Carmichael

* * *

LIFE

Life is that existence that is given to man to live for a purpose, to live to his own satisfaction and pleasure, providing he forgets not the God who created him and who expects a spiritual obedience and observation of the moral laws that he inspired.

--Marcus Garvey

Life is something like the trumpet. If you don't put anything in it you don't get anything out. And that's the truth.

--W. C. Handy

How to solve life's saddest problems,
Its weariness, want and woe, was answered by one who suffered
In Palestine long ago.

--Francis E. W. Harper

Life for me ain't no crystal stair.

--Langston Hughes

My life, almost from its very start, has been filled with
tragedy and romance, failure and success, poverty and wealth,
misery and happiness.

--Jack Johnson

The height of life is the upward search for God.

--Martin Luther King Jr.

The end of life is to do the will of God, come what may.

--Martin Luther King Jr.
The Christian Century

Life should be strong and complete on every side. Any
complete life has . . . three dimensions . . . length, breadth,
and height.

--Martin Luther King Jr.

All life is inter-related. Whatever affects one of us affects
us all.

--Martin Luther King Jr.

The breath of life is the inward drive to achieve one's
personal ends and ambitions, an inward concern for one's own
welfare and achievements.

--Martin Luther King Jr.

A life is not important except in the impact it has on others
lives.

--Jackie Robinson

The miracle of a man's life is life itself.

--Howard Thurman

Life is a compromise.
The important thing is not to be so stubborn that you don't give
an inch.

--Barbara M. Watson

* * *

LISTEN

What a happy country this will be, if whites will listen

--David Walker

* * *

LIVE

When you live for today, you die for tomorrow.

--Black Maxim

* * *

LIVING

The secret of live is to live, and I've lived, baby.

--Adam Clayton Powell Jr.

* * *

LONGEVITY

It does not matter how long you have but how you live.

--Martin Luther King Jr.

The Lord made me out of good dirt.

--Arthur Reed
Reputed 123 years old

       *   *   *

LORD

The Lord will make a way somehow.

--Black Maxim

The good Lord takes care of fools and babies.

--Black Maxim

Precious Lord take my hand,
Lead me on, let me stand,
I am tired, I am weak, I am worn.
Through the storm, through the night,
Lead me on to the light
Take my hand precious Lord, lead me home.

--Thomas Dorsey

With the power of the Lord with me I can't be defeated.

--Marilyn McCoo

       *   *   *

LOST

There is only one thing, on disenchantment. . . . It is impossible to get lost in a crowd.

--Wilt Chamberlain

       *   *   *

LOVE

It is better to be loved than feared.

--African Proverb

___

Dine with a stranger but save your love for your family.

--African Proverb

___

If you love the children of others, you will love your own even better.

--Afro American

___

Never love something or someone who cannot love you in return.

--Black Maxim

___

I love you once,
I love you twice,
I love you next to red beans and rice.

--Black Saying

___

Do I love you with all my heart
I love you with my liver;
An if I had you in my mouth
I'd spit you in the river.

--Black Saying

___

I loves my gal,
She ain't no goose
Blacker 'an blackberries,
Sweeter 'an juice.

--Black Saying

___

Anything will give up its secrets if you love it enough.

--George Wasington Carver

___

When loves chains upon thee lie
Bid all happiness goodbye.

--Creole Love Song

We cannot hold our love, but there is one love that neer
changeth or is mistaken, and that is God's.

--Marcus Garvey

I still believe that love is the most durable power in the
world. Over the centuries men have sought to discover the highest
good.
He who loves is a participant in the being of God. He who
hates does not know God.

--Martin Luther King Jr.

As I delved deeper into the philosophy of Gandhi my skepticism
concerning the power of love gradually diminished and I came to
see for the first time that the christian doctrine of love
operating through the Gandhian method of nonviolence was one of
the most potent weapons available to oppressed people in their
struggle for freedom.

--Martin Luther King Jr.

Love never let me down.

--Anwar el-Sadat

Love is a human safeguard against all social pitfalls.

--Anwar el-Sadat

A man does not seek luck, luck seeks its man.

--Afro American

* * *

LUNACY

There are forty kinds of lunacy, but only one kind of common sense.

--Black Maxim

*   *   *

M

MAN

Man has created a generation of guided missiles and misguided men.

--Martin Luther King Jr.

I am an invisible man. No, I am not a spook like those who haunted Edgar Allan Poe; nor am I one of your Hollywood- movie ectoplasms. I am a man of substance, of flesh and bone fiber and liquids- and I might even be said to possess a mind. I am invisible, understand, simply because people refuse to see.

--Ralph Ellison

It is the little man who looks for the worst- and finds it.

--Samuel Coleridge Taylor

*   *   *

MANSIONS

Those bright mansions above,
  Bright Mansions above;
Lord, I want to live up yonder,
  In bright mansions above.

--Afro American

* * *

MARCHING

We're for marches in the Urban League . . . We need to march
to the polling places, march our kids to the library, march to
P.T.A. meetings. We need to march as men, Black men, into the
ghetto and meet some of those little boys who have no father, and
be cub scout leaders for them and set up Little League (baseball)
teams and be substitute fathers.

--Whitney Young Jr.

* * *

MASK

We wear the mask.

--Paul Laurence Dunbar

* * *

MASTER

Jimmy crack corn
And I don't care
My master is gone away.

--Slave Saying

* * *

MATERIAL

There's a wealth of still unwritten material about the
Negro--life on a Negro College campus, for example--that I won't
run out of material for 50 years.

--Langston Hughes

*   *   *

MEDITATION

Let the words of our mouths and the meditation of our hearts
be acceptable in Thy Sight,
O 'Lord, our strength and our Redeemer.

--Black Church Service Meditation

*   *   *

MELTING POT

I hear that melting pot stuff a lot, and all I can say is that
we haven't melted.

--Jesse   Jackson

_____

The United States is the melting pot of the world--the colored
man either did not get into the pot or didn't get melted down.

--Thurgood Marshall

*   *   *

MEN

If it is dark all men are black.

--African Proverb

_____

The Crazy Man and the Greasy Man will get you!

--Black Folklore

*   *   *

MIGHT

Might cannot fight against wealth and wisdom.

--Marcus Garvey

*   *   *

MIND

Got one mind for the white folk to see
Nother one for what I know is me.

--Slave Saying

*   *   *

MINISTRY

My call to the ministry was not dramatic. . . . It was my
final realization of an inner urge to serve God and humanity. It
was a response to an inescapable challenge.

--Martin Luther King Jr.

*   *   *

MINORITY

Almost always the creative, dedicated minority has made the
world better.

--Martin Luther King Jr.

*   *   *

MISCEGENATION

It's too late for the white people to get excited about the mingling of the races. They should have got excited in 1619 when the first female slaves landed in this country.

--Benjamin Mays

* * *

MISTAKES

If a doctor is mistaken he leaves by the back of the house.

--African Proverb

* * *

MOB

The mob has many heads, but no brains.

--African Proverb

* * *

MODESTY

A too modest man goes hungry.

--African Proverb

* * *

MOJO

```
No power can stay the mojo
    When the obi is purple
    And the vodu is green
And shango is whispering
    Bathe me in blood
    I am not clean.
```

--Henry Dumas

* * *

MONEY

Money is sharper than a sword.

--African Proverb

─────────

Well I, I live in the realm of art and have no monetary
interests.

--Duke Ellington

─────────

Money talks, bullshit can take a walk.

--Black Saying

─────────

You can keep your Rhodes Scholars, we don't want the money
that come from the sweat of our people.

--Stokely Carmichael

* * *

MOTHER

```
O' mother, don't you weep when I'm gone.
For I'm going to Heav'n above,
Going to the God I love.
```

--Black Spiritual

─────────

Mom, this is my last fight.

> --Joe Louis
> Statement Made After Each Fight

O, where has mother gone, papa?
What makes you so sad?
Why sit you here alone, papa?
Has anyone made you mad?
O, tell me, dear papa,
Has master punished you again?
Shall I go bring the salt, papa,
To rub your back and cure the pain?

> --W.H. Robinson

* * *

MULATTO

Mulatto, one half black, white and Negro;
Quateron (Quadroon), one fourth black, white and mulatto;
Metis, or Metif, one-eighth black, white and quarteron;
Meamelouc, one sixteenth black, white and metis;
Demi- meamelouc, one thirty second black, white and meamelouc;
Griffe, three fourths black, Negro and mulatto;
Sacratra, seven eighths black, Griffe and Negro.

All these variations exist in New Orleans, and experts pretend to
be able to distinguish them.

> --Afro American

My old man died in a fine big house.
My ma died in a shack.
I wonder where I'am going to die,
Being neither white nor black.

> --Langston Hughes

As soon as a mulatto is able to own a horse, he will tell his
mother he isn't a nigger.

> --Creole Slave Saying

* * *

MUSIC

Up above my head I hear, music in the air,
There must be a God somewhere.

--Black Spiritual

_____

Music is the woman you always wanted to find.

--Duke Ellington

_____

In a popular form, Negro music, launched by white men- not
Negroes has swept the world.

--Paul Robeson

_____

Music is in my mouth,
 Laughing, crying on my tongue,
Glad music, sad music,
 All taking form
In spiritual and blues.

--J. Washington Haines

_____

What Brahms has done for the Hungarian folk-music, Dvorak for
the Bohemian, and Greg for the Norwegian, I have tried to do for
these Negro Melodies.

--Samuel Coleridge Taylor

* * *

N

NAME

Nobody in America knows my real name, and if I can prevent it, nobody ever will.

--Bert Williams

*   *   *

NAT TURNER

He stood erect, a man Doomed to a life of plodding toil,
Shamefully rooted to the soil.
He stood erect, his eyes flashed fire;
His robust form convulsed with ire;
"I will be free! I will be free!
cried he.

--T. Thomas Fortune

*   *   *

NATION

The ruin of a nation begins in the homes of its people.

--African Proverb

*   *   *

NEGRO

Please stop using the word Negro. We are the only human beings in the world with fifty-seven variety of complexions who are classed together as a single unit.

--Mary Church Terrell

* * *

NEGRO WOMAN

The sky hangs heavy to-night
Like the hair of a Negro Woman

The stars twinkle-to-night
Like the glaze of a Negro Woman's eyes,

Drinking the tears set flowing by an aging hurt
Gnawing at her heart.

--Opportunity Magazine
Alexander Lewis

* * *

NEIGHBOR

Love Thy Neighbor is a precept which could transform the world if it were universally practiced.

--Mary Mcleod Bethune

* * *

NEW ORLEANS

I suppose you've heard how New Orleans
Is famed for wealth and beauty;
There's girls of ever hue, it seems,
   From snowy white to sooty.

--Anglo African Magazine

* * *

NIGHTMARE

Having a nightmare while sleeping on your back means a witch is riding your back.

--Black Folklore

* * *

NOBILITY

That is why, in the nobility of man, he is matchless, that is why, though still by death, he lives.

--Harry Belafonte
Stanley Levinson
Tribute to Martin Luther King Jr.

* * *

NON-COOPERATION

I have become convinced then that non-cooperation with evil is as much a moral obligation as is cooperation with good.

--Martin Luther King Jr.

* * *

O

OLD

I am no more the ardent love,
Who caused the world such vast amaze;
My spring is past, my summer over,
And dead the fires of other days.
Oh, Eros, God of youth: your servant
was loyal-that you will avow. Could I be born
again this moment, Ah, with what zest I'd serve you now.

                                    --Alexander Pushkin

* * *

OPPRESSION

Suffer me to recall to your mind that time in which the arms
and tyranny of the British Crown were exerted with every powerful
effort in order to reduce you to a state of servitude.
This, sir, was a time when you cleraly saw into the injustice
of a state of slavery and in which you had just apprehensions of
the horrors of its conditions.

                                    --Benjamin Banneker
                                      Letter to Thomas Jefferson

                     ————

You can't hold a good man down without staying down with him.

                                    --Booker T. Washington

                     ————

Out of the depths of oppression to the heights of freedom.

--Anonymous

*　*　*

ORGANIZATION

Organization is a great power in directing the affairs of a race or nation toward a given goal.

--Marcus Garvey

*　*　*

OUTCAST

I have no protection at home, or resting place abroad. . . . I am an outcast from the society of my childhood, an outlaw in the land of my birth. I am a stranger with thee, and a sojourner as all my fathers were.

--Frederick Douglass

*　*　*

OUTHOUSE

All newspapers used in the outhouse have good news.

--Black Folk Saying

*　*　*

OVERCOME

We Shall Overcome.

--Horton, Seeger, Hamilton, Caravan

*　*　*

OWN

Mama may have, papa may have, but God bless the child that's got his own.

--Billie Holliday

*   *   *

OWNERSHIP

In America everything is owned. . . . Until recently, the blacks themselves were counted as part of somebody's private property, along with the chickens and the goats.

--Eldridge Cleaver

*   *   *

P

PAIN

Life is full of sin, sorrow, and pain.

--Slave Saying

* * *

PASSING

I'm told that there are in America today between two and five million "white Negroes" who are "passing" in white society. Imagine their torture! Living in constant fear that some black person they've known might meet and expose them. Imagine every day living a lie.

--Malcolm X

* * *

PASSION

The best passion is compassion.

--Jamaican

Human passion is the hallucination of a distempered mind.

>   --William Whipper

* * *

PAST

Don't look back
Something might be gaining on you.

>   --Satchel Paige

* * *

PATIENCE

At the bottom of patience there is heaven.

>   --African Proverb

_____

When somebody's choking me to death, that's no reason to talk about patience.

>   --Thurgood Marshall

* * *

PEACE

A woman's clothes are the price of her husband's peace.

>   --African Proverb

_____

Peace is much more precious than a piece of land.

>   --Anwar el-Sadat

* * *

PEN

The pen is the holiest implement created by man

        --Anwar el-Sadat

*   *   *

PEOPLE

We surely must be concerned about people on the outside who want to be on the inside.

        --Jesse Jackson

*   *   *

PERSEVERENCE

Perseverence is everything.

        --African Proverb

_____

Perseverence brings success.

        --Afro American

*   *   *

POINT

The point of the needle is the easiest end to find.

        --Black Aphorism

*   *   *

POLITICAL POWER

Political power may well, in the days to come, be the most effective tool of the Negro's liberation.

--Martin Luther King Jr.

* * *

POLITICIANS

I find that politicians are able to fool the public better than actors can. It isn't that they act better, it's just that they have a non-paying audience standing there hoping for something- promises that can never be kept by one man.

--Pearl Bailey

_____

I have learned that independence and integrity are not the most desirable attributes in politicians- although they should be.

--Shirley Chisholm

_____

Politicians have always exploited black people

--Clint Newton

* * *

POLITICS

At best, politics is not inspiring.

--Jack Johnson

_____

Republicans start depressions and Democrats start wars.

--Black Satirical Saying

_____

Blacks will no longer settle for being the Harlem
Globetrotters of the Democratic Party.

--Jesse Jackson

Politics is no box of crackerjacks, it is not candy and
popcorn and free prizes.

--Carl Stokes

U.S. politics is ruled by special interest blocs and lobbies.

--Malcolm X

* * *

POOR

The poor man and the rich man do not play together.

--African Proverb

* * *

POTENTIAL

I mean we've all got possibilities, capacities for
attainment. I don't in the least minimize what I am up against as
a Negro. I have less to buck against as a lawyer.

--Paul Robeson

* * *

POVERTY

Poverty makes free man become slaves.

--African Proverb

There is nothing like poverty for taking the conceit out of a man.

                                        --African Proverb

                    _____

Poverty is slavery.

                                        --African Proverb

                    _____

The marriage of paupers only increases beggars.

                                        Afro American

                    _____

No one is poor but he who thinks himself so.

                                        --Afro American

                    _____

Poverty isn't a screw; but it's a very long nail.

                                        --Creole Slave Proverb

                    _____

Poverty destroys pride. It is difficult for an empty bag to stand upright.

                                        --Alexandre Dumas fils

                    _____

A hellish state to be in. It is no virtue. It is a crime.

                                        --Marcus Garvey

                    _____

The time has come for an all-out world war against poverty.

                                        --Martin Luther King Jr.

                    *   *   *

POWER

A powerful friend becomes a powerful enemy.

                                        --African Proverb

                    _____

The more powerful one is in this world, the more servile one will be in the next.

--African Proverb

Power concedes nothing without demands- it never did and it never will.

Frede rick Douglass

Power is the only argument that satisfies man.

--Marcus Garvey

The only protection against injustice in man is power-physical, financial and scientific.

--Marcus Garvey

Excrement isn't sharp, but it makes you limp.

--Haitian Proverb

Power, properly understood, is the ability to achieve purpose.

--Martin Luther King Jr.

Black people must seek audacious power--the kind of power which cradles your head amongst the stars and gives you the security to stand up as proud men and women, eyeball to eyeball with the rest of the world.

--Adam Clayton Powell Jr.

Black power is black responsibility.

--Adam Clayton Powell Jr.

Only power can effect the enforcement and adoption of a given policy, however meritoricus it may be.

--A. Phillip Randolph

I have never sought power; for early in my life I discovered that my strength lies within me- in my absolute devotion to what is right, just, and beautiful.

--Anwar el-Sadat

The love of power is one of the greatest human infirmities, and with it comes the upsurping influence of despotism, the mother of slavery.

--William Whipper

* * *

PRAYER

Don't pray when it's raining if you don't pray when the sun is shining.

--Satchel Paige

* * *

PREJUDICE

The entire absence of prejudice in Europe is one of the clearest proofs that the hatred of the colored person owes solely to the overpowering influence of slavery.

--William Wells Brown

The discovery of personal whiteness among the world's peoples is a very modern thing,--a nineteenth century matter, indeed. The ancient world would have laughed at such a distinction.

--W.E.B. Dubois

I have found no better way of avoiding racial prejudice than to act in my relations with people of other races as if prejudice did not exist.

--Jack Johnson

Plant next to prejudice, another tree that grows so big and high that discrimination has to wither and die.

--Jessie Owens

* * *

PRESIDENT

A white boy may sit with me watching the President on television, and think: I could be President. No such thought would have occurred to this black boy or any other. In fact the white boy is wrong: he doesn't have much chance either of becoming President. Unless he has money, the right contacts or education; he too will be excluded.

--Stokely Carmichael

* * *

PRIDE

Say it Loud. I am Black and I am Proud.

--James Brown

The proud black spirit seeks justice and decency.

--Whitney Young Jr.

* * *

PROBLEMS

No problem should ever be regarded as insuperable.

--Anwar el-Sadat

* * *

PRODUCT

The Negro is made and manufactured in America.

--Ron Karenga

*   *   *

PROGRESS

Actually, I don't think man's made much progress- other than scientific progess- since Biblical days.

--Ray Charles

———

Looking back over what I've heard and seen, I can't say I've witnesses progress in the world. If you tie up my hands and then release one finger, I don't call that progress.

--Ray Charles

———

If there is no struggle, there is no progress.

--Frederick Douglass

———

It's time to move from the outhouse to the White House.

--Jesse Jackson

———

A few crumbs for a few is too often hailed as progress for the race.

--Paul Robeson

———

Blacks have come a long way, but you have to remember that they started out with a disadvantage that dates back to slavery. Our standards come down from our ancestors. You can look at it this way: Look how far we have come. But look how far they have gone.

--John Thompson

*   *   *

PROMISE

A promise is a debt.

--African Proverb

* * *

PROMISED LAND

Like anybody I would like to live a long life. Longevity has
its grace. But I'm not concerned about that now. I just want to
do God's will. And he's allowed me to go up to the mountain, and
I've looked over, and I've seen the Promised Land.
I may not get there with you. But I want you to know tonight
that we as a people will get to the Promised Land!
So I'm happy tonight! I'm not fearing any man: mine eyes
have seen the glory of the coming of the Lord.

--Martin Luther King Jr.

_____

I'll meet you in the morning
Safe in the Promised Land
On the other side of Jordan!
Bound for the Promised Land.

--Slave Saying

* * *

PROSTITUTION

Old women working by an age old plan to make bread in ways as
best they can.

--Margaret Walker

* * *

PROTEST

It is better to protest than to accept injustice.

--Rosa Parks

————

Protest- the right of protest- is basic to a democratic form of government. The right of petition; the right of assembly; the right of freedom of speech are so basic to our government that they are enshrined in the very first amendment to the Constitution. And the 14th Amendment says that no state shall throttle these freedoms.

--Thurgood Marshall

* * *

PROVERBS

Proverbs are the daughters of experience.

--African Proverb

————

A wise man who knows proverbs, reconciles difficulties.

--African Proverb

* * *

PUNISHMENT

There is scarcely a single fact more worthy of indelible record, than the utter inefficiency of human punishments, to cure human evils.

--William Whipper

* * *

Q

QUADROON

 Yellow girl goes to the ball;
Nigger lights her to the hall.
                Fiddler man?
Now, what is that to you?
Say, what is that to you?
Fiddler man?

--Creole Slave Song

* * *

R

RACE

If you're white, you're right
If you're brown, stick around
If you're black, get back.

--Black Saying

_____

Our race and color are not of our own choosing. The only
excuse for pride in individuals or race is in the fact of their
achievements. Our color is the gift of the Almighty. We should
neither be proud of it nor ashamed of it.

--Frederick Douglass

_____

The Negro race, like all races, is going to be saved by its
exceptional men.

--W.E.B. Dubois

_____

A race without authority and power, is a race without respect.

--Marcus Garvey

_____

At best, race is a superstition.

--George S. Schuyler

* * *

RACISM

Racism is real enough in the United States, but exclusion is not based on race alone.

--Stokely Carmichael

_____

Meeting and beating racism is positive militancy.

--Clifton R. Wharton Jr.

*   *   *

RAGE

Black people are enraged because there are social injustices which provoke rage.

--Bayard Rustin

*   *   *

RAPE

It was because white America needed cheap or free labor that she raped our African homeland of millions of black people.

--Stokely Carmichael

_____

A people raped of a country
A people raped of a homeland
A people raped of a tradition
A people raped of a heritage
A people raped of a culture.

--Judith Burton

*   *   *

READING

Reading is to the mind what eating is to the body.

--Afro American

* * *

REASON

The power of reason is the noblest gift of heaven to man,
because it assimilates man to his maker.

--William Whipper

* * *

RECOGNITION

I want to be known as a poet, not as a Negro poet.

--Countee Cullen

* * *

REDEMPTION

I have lived these last few years with the conviction that
unearned suffering is redemptive.

--Martin Luther King Jr.

* * *

RELIGION

Religion originated with the colored peoples. Four thousand
years before Abraham wandered from his home in far off Ur, black
men had worshipped God as such.

--The Spokesman Magazine

We must face the shameful fact that all too many religious
people have been religious in their creed but not enough in their
deeds.

--Martin Luther King Jr.

We might as well settle down to the uncompromising fact that
our people will grow in proportion as we teach them that the way
to have the most of Jesus and in a permanent form is to mix with
their religion some land, cotton, and corn, a house with two or
three rooms, and a little bank account.

--Booker T. Washington

* * *

REMEDY

There is a salve for every sore.

--Afro American

* * *

REPARATIONS

We are therefore demanding of the white Christian churches and
Jewish Synagogues which are part and parcel of the system of
capitalism, that they begin to pay reparations to black people in
this country. We are demanding $500 million from the Christian
white churches and the Jewish Synagogues. This total comes to $15
per nigger. This is a low estimate, for we maintain there are
probably more than 30,000,000 black people in this country.

--James Forman

* * *

REPUTATION

Leave a good name behind in case you return.

--Afro American Encyclopedia

* * *

RESPECT

Familiarity breeds contempt; distance breeds respect.

--African Proverb

It'll take another twenty five, thirty or forty years for people of different races to respect each other in this country- if ever.

--Ray Charles

The respect that is bought by gold is not worth much.

--Frances Harper

Respect is key to all human relationships.

--Black Maxim

I can honestly say I have never worked to be liked, I have worked only to be respected.

--Bill Russell

* * *

REVISION

The American Negro must remake his past in order to make his future.

--Arthur Schomburg

* * *

REWARD

No man who continues to add something to the material, intellectual and moral well-being to the place in which he lives is left without proper reward.

--Booker T. Washington

* * *

RICH

She even thinks in heaven
Her class lies late and snores
While poor black cherubs rise at seven
To do celestial chores.

--Countee Cullen

* * *

RIGHTS

I know of no rights of race superior to the rights of humanity.

--Ralph Bunche

_____

A Chief Justice of the Supreme Court of the United States once said: "The Negro has no rights which the white man is bound to respect," still underlies many of the dealings of the white race with the black.

--Paul Robeson

* * *

RIVER

A river is never too wide to cross.

--Black Maxim

_____

There's a lot of Black folks buried in the Mississippi River.

--Black Saying

_____

My soul has grown deep like the Rivers.

--Langston Hughes

_____

I am the River Niger-hear my waters!
I am totally flexible.
I am the River Niger-hear
My waters are the first sperm of the world.
When the earth was but a faceless whistling embryo
Life burst from my liquid kernels like popcorn.

--Joseph A. Walker

RUMBLE

Float like a butterfly
Sting like a bee
Rumble young man, Rumble.

--Muhammad Ali

*   *   *

S

SACRIFICE

In any country there must be people who have to die. They are
the sacrifices any nation has to make to achieve law and order.

--Idi Amin

He gave his life in search of a more excellent way, a more
effective way, a creative rather than a destructive way. We
intend to go on in search of that way, and I hope that you who
loved and admired him would join us in fulfilling his dream.

--Coretta Scott King

*   *   *

SATAN

Satan lives!

--Black Maxim

Old Satan loves a big crowd.

--Black Saying

*   *   *

SATISFACTION

My people will never be satisfied until they see black faces in high places.

--Mary McLeod Bethune

       *   *   *

SCAPEGOAT

The fear of me made all men cease their bickerings
And I became the scapegoat of the nation.

--Marcus Christian

       *   *   *

SEGREGATION

Segregation is on its deathbed- the question now is, how costly will the segregationists make the funeral?

--Martin Luther King Jr.

Segregation is the offspring of an illicit intercourse between injustice and immorality.

--Martin Luther King Jr.

I got the feeling (from what has been said here) that when you put a white child in a school with a whole lot of colored children, the child would fall apart or something. Everybody knows that is not true. Those same kids in Virginia and South Carolina--and I have seen them do it--they play in the streets together, they play on their farms together, they go down the road together, they separate to go to school, they come out of school and play ball together. They have to be separated in school. . . . Why of all the multitudinous groups of people in this country do you have to single out Negroes and give them this separate treatment?

--Thurgood Marshall
Oral Arguments Brown Vs Board of Ed.

In all things that are social, we can be as separate as the fingers, yet one as the hand in all things essential to mutual progress.

--Booker T Washington

* * *

SELF ACCEPTANCE

Sometimes I think I am the only Negro living who would not prefer to be white. What would have become of the genius of Marie Lloyd if she had been ashamed of being Cockney?
Would Robert Burns have been as great a poet if he had denied his poughman speech and aped the gentlemen of his day.

--Paul Robeson

No Negro will leave a permanent mark on the world till he learns to be true to himself.

--Paul Robeson

* * *

SELFISHNESS

No universal selfishness can bring social good to all.

--W.E.B. Dubois

* * *

SEPARATION

There is no separation of "law" from politics.

--H. Rap Brown

* * *

SERVITUDE

The universal triumph of the Negro in Art and in Sport constitutes the second step of his servitude. It is quite just that each follows his own vocation, but if we do not have more than art, literature and athletics, our future will be very precarious- for the present and the future belong principally to technology and the machine.

--Gustano E. Urrutia

*   *   *

SEXISM

I never understood the magnitude of racism, until I understood the magnitude of my sexism.

--Dick Gregory

*   *   *

SHAKE

Look at that gal
   Shake that thing
We cannot all be
   Martin Luther King.

--Julian Bond

*   *   *

SHAME

Ashamed of my race?
And of what race am I?
I am many in one.
Through my veins there flows the blood of Red men,
  Black men, Briton, Celt and Scot,
In warring clash and tumultuous riot.
I welcome all,
But love the blood of the kindly race
That swarthes my skin, crinkles my hair,
And puts sweet music in my soul.

--Joseph Cotter, Jr.

_____

This country has been able to make us ashamed of being black.

--Stokely Carmichael

* * *

SICKNESS

He who conceals his disease cannot expect to be cured.

--African Proverb

_____

When you recover from sickness, don't forget about God.

--African Proverb

* * *

SIN

The biggest sin is sitting on your ass.

--Florynce Kennedy

* * *

SING

Lift every voice and sing
Till earth and heaven ring,
Ring with the harmonies of liberty;
Let our rejoicing rise
High as the listening skies,
Let it resound loud as the rolling sea.

Sing a song full of the faith that the dark past has taught us,
Sing a song full of hope that the present has brought us,
Facing the rising sun of our new day begun
Let us march on till victory is won.

--James Weldon Johnson

* * *

SLAVE

    Were I a slave, I would be free, I would not live to live as a
slave, But boldly strike for Liberty, For Freedom or a martyr's
grave.

--Martin Delaney

_____

"Master, said the dying bondsman
 "Home and friends I soon shall see;
But before I reach my country,
 Master, write that I am free.

For the spirits of my fathers
 would shrink back from me in pride,
If I told them at our greeting
 I a slave had lived and died.

--Frances Harper

_____

    I would never be any service to anyone as a slave.

--Nat Turner

* * *

SLAVERY

  See wives and husbands torn apart
Their childrens screams, they grieve my heart.
  They are torn away to Georgia!
Come go along with me-
  They are torn away to Georgia!
Go sound the Jubilee.

                            --Martin R. Delaney

  I'm on my way to Canada,
That cold and dreary land;
The dire effects of slavery,
  I can no longer stand.
My soul is vexed within me so,
  To think that I'm a slave,
I've now resolved to strike the blow,
  For freedom or the grave.

                            --Martin R. Delaney

    The first object which saluted my eyes when I arrived on the
coast was the sea, and a slave ship, which was then riding at
anchor, and waiting for its cargo. These filled me with
astonishment, which was soon converted into terror, when I was
carried on board I was immediately handled, and tossed up, to see
if I were sound, by some of the crew, and I was now persuaded that
I had gone into a world of bad spirits, and that they were going
to kill me. Their complexion too differing so much from ours,
their long hair, and the language they spoke (which was different
from any I had ever heard) united to confirm me in this belief.

                            --Olaudah Equiano

The Sale began- young girls were there,
  Defenseless in their wretchedness
Whose stifled sobs of deep despair
  Revealed their anguish and distress.

And mothers stood with streaming eyes,
  And saw their dearest children sold;
Unheeded rose their bitter cries,
  While tyrants bartered them for gold.

                            --Frances Harper

Alas! and am I born for this,
  To wear this slavish chain?
Deprived of all created bliss,
  Through hardship toil and pain!

How long have I in bondage lain,
  and languished to be free.
Alas! and must I still complain--
  Deprived of liberty.

Oh heaven! and is there no relief
  This side the silent grave--
To soothe the pain- to quell the grief,
  And anguish of a slave?

                              --George M. Horton

————

    My ole mistress promise me w'en she died, she'd set me free.
She lived so long dat 'er head got bal, An' she give out de notion
a dyin at all.

                              --Harlem Quarterly

————

    Slavery was tough, boss. You just don't know how tough it was.

                              --Tiner Hendricks
                                Ex-Slave

————

    Slave owners were wrong when they thought that slaves had no
idea of what freedom means. The slaves it well enough- they can
compare themselves with the white men and see the difference
between working for someone else and working for yourself.

                              --Solomon Northrup

————

In New Orleans famed market place I stood,
In Baltimore, Savannah, Louisville,
Straining mulatto babies to my breast,
Torrents of throttled pleas dawned in my throat,
While calloused owners bartered them and me
To satisfy a pressing gambling debt.

                              --Ethel Clark Riley

————

No, I can never forget 300 odd years of slavery and
half-freedom; the long, weary and bitter years of degradation
visited upon our mothers and sisters, the humiliation and Jim
Crowing of a whole people.

--Paul Robeson

I kept my eye on the north star, and thought of liberty.

--Slave Saying

Before I'd be a slave
I'd be buried in my grave and go home to my Lord and be free.

--Black Spiritual

Black Americans were the only racial or ethnic group brought
to America against their will.

--Thomas Sowell

Oh my poor Nellie Grey
They have taken her away
And I'll never see my darling any more
I am sitting by the river
And I am weeping all the day
For You've gone from the old Kentucky Home.

One night I went to see her
But 'she's gone the neighbors say,
The white man has bound her with his chain
They have taken her to Georgia
To wear her life away
As she toils her life away
As she toils in the cotton and the cane,
Oh my darling Nellie Grey.

--Slave Saying

Slavery and freedom
They mostly the same
No difference hardly
Except in de name.

--Former Slave Statement

Like birds, for others we have built the downy nest;
Like sheep, for others we have won the fleecy vest,
Like bees, for others we have collected the honeyed food;
Like the patient ox, we have labored for others good.

--George H. White

_____

My children, France comes to make us slaves. God gave us
liberty; France has no right to take it away. Burn the cities,
destroy the harvests, tear up the roads with cannon, poison the
wells, show the white man the hell he comes to make.

--Toussaint L'Ouverture

* * *

SLAVES

Slaves are expected to sing as well as work.

--Frederick Douglass

_____

You had far better all die- die immediately, than live slaves,
and entail you wretchedness upon you posterity.

--Henry Highland Garnet

_____

Better even die free, than to live slaves.

--Frederick Douglass

_____

Negro slaves thus became the creators of the wealth that made
the flowering of capitalism possible in the nineteenth century.

--Eric Williams

* * *

SLEEP

Sleep is the cousin of death.

--African Proverb

*   *   *

SLOTH

Sloth is the key to poverty.

--African Proverb

*   *   *

SMILE

The amount of happiness produced simply by wearing a smiling
face, is incalculable.

--Adah Issacs Menken

*   *   *

SMOKE

I am the smoke king,
I am black.

--W.E.B. Dubois

*   *   *

SOCIALISM

Black people are the lowest on the economic ladder and the function of that structure is precisely to insure that exploitation. Socialism is the only thing that can provide the answer.

--Angela Davis

* * *

SOMEBODY

I am Somebody
I may be poor, but I am Somebody
I am Somebody!
I may be hungry, but I am Somebody.
I am Somebody!

--Jesse Jackson

* * *

SON

A good son makes a good husband.

--Afro American

* * *

SOUL FOOD

The reason I catch so many fish is because I feed them just what they like . . . grits, eggs, pork chops and chitterlings.

--Satchel Paige

* * *

SOULS

Yes, our souls have been tried in the cold and bitter Valley Forges of the deep south, and black and white together, we have met the test. We shall overcome.

--Martin Luther King Jr.

* * *

SOUTH

O Southland, dear Southland!
Then why do you still cling
To an idle age and a musty sage,
To a dead and useless thing?

--James Weldon Johnson

* * *

SOUTH AFRICA

I find it difficult to understand the mentality of these racists of South Africa. Their entire wealth rests upon non-European labour.

--Paul Robeson

* * *

SPARK

Events in history occur when the time has ripened for them, but they need a spark. Little Rock was that spark at that stage of the struggle of the American Negro for justice.

--Daisy Bates

* * *

SPIRITUALS

In his spirituals the Negro expressed his conception of the creation of man and the mystery of death and the hope of a better fate beyond the grave.

--E. Franklin Frazier

The spirituals reflected, on the whole, the philosophy of life of the Negro folk.

--E. Franklin Frazier

I have sometimes thought, that the mere hearing of these songs would do more to impress truly spiritual-minded men and women with the soul crushing and death-dealing character of slavery, than the reading of whole volumes of its mere physical cruelties. They speak to the heart and to the soul of the thoughtful.

--Frederick Douglass

Spirituals portray the hopes of our people who faced the hardships of slavery. . . . They sang to forget the chains and misery. The sorry will one day turn to joy. All that breaks the heart and oppresses the soul will one day give place to peace and understanding, and every man will be free. That is the interpretation of a true Negro spiritual.

--Paul Robeson

* * *

STAND

Whenever you take a stand for truth and justice, you are liable to scorn.

--Martin Luther King Jr.

* * *

STARDOM

There is the possibility that Southern audiences might object to me, not as a film actor (I suppose I could do small parts) but as a film star. They would resent the knowledge that a Negro was enjoying the social and economic advantage of the star's position.

--Paul Robeson

* * *

STEAL

He who learns to steal must learn to run.

--Afro American

* * *

STUPIDITY

He who is stupid tramples thrice on excrement.

--African Proverb

* * *

SUCCEED

The only way you can succeed is to over ride the obstacles in your way.

--Frederick Douglass

* * *

SUCCESS

One who has seen a thousand cannot be satisfied with a hundred.

--African Proverb

————

There is no force like success, and that is why the individual makes all efforts to surround himself throughout life with the evidence of it.

--Marcus Garvey

————

It's not easy to make it . . . but I do say that in America, everything is possible.

--Daniel "Chappie" James

————

I guess my formula for success is picking attainable goals, then achieving them. Once you have achieved one goal, the success will give you the confidence to reach the next.

--John H. Johnson

————

It means so little when a man like me wins some success. Where is the benefit when a small class of Negroes make money and can live well? It may be encouraging, but it has no deeper significance.
I feel this way because I have cousins who can neither read nor write. I have had a chance. They have not. That is the difference.

--Paul Robeson

————

And I say to the New York Times that personal success can be no answer. It can no longer be a question of an Anderson, a Garver, a Robinson, a Jackson, or a Robeson. It must be a question of the well-being and opportunities not of a few but for all of this great Negro people of which I am a part.

--Paul Robeson

————

I never had it made.

--Jackie Robinson

————

The individual who can do something that the world wants will,
in the end, make his way regardless of race.

--Booker T. Washington

*   *   *

SUFFERING

Our suffering is our bridge to one another.

--James Baldwin

Neither God, nor angels, or just men, command you to suffer
for a single moment.

--Henry Highland Garnet

*   *   *

SUPERIORITY

A brilliant Negro essayist has suggested that the Negro's
greatest gift to America is his creation in the American white of
a very deep-rooted "superiority complex" and that those qualities
of American self-assurance which too often find unworthy
expression in bumptiousness and an agressive reluctance to be
disciplined, are partly founded on the consciousness which is the
birthright of every American, that, however poor a fellow may be,
there is always a caste, a whole race of men, to whom he has
inherited a contemptuous superiority.

--Paul Robeson

*   *   *

T

TALK

He who talks incessantly, talks nonsense.

--African Proverb

_____

A chattering bird builds no nest.

--African Proverb

*   *   *

TEMPTATION

When a woman lifts her dress, the devil looks at her leg.

--Creole Proverb

*   *   *

TESTAMENT

I was an Israelite walking a sea bottom,
I was a Negro slave following the North Star,
I was an immigrant huddled in a ship's belly,
I was a Mormon searching for a temple,
I was a refugee clogging roads to nowhere--
Always the dream was freedom.

--Pauli Murray

* * *

THIEF

A known thief is always under suspicion.

--African Proverb

* * *

TIME

How long, O Lord, how long?

--Black Spiritual

Seize the time!

--Bobby Seale

* * *

TIRED

I am so tired and weary,
  So tired of the endless fight,
So weary of waiting the dawn
  And finding endless night.

That I asked but rest and quiet-
  Rest for the days that are gone,
And quiet for the little space
  That I must journey on.

--Joseph Cotler Jr.

_____

   I am tired of work; I am tired of building up somebody else's
civilization.

--Fenton Johnson

_____

I am tired of sailing my little boat
Far inside the harbor bar
I want to go out where the big ships float
Out on the deep where the great ones are.
And should my frail craft prove too slight
For waves that sweep those billows o'er
I'd rather go down in the stirring fight
Than drowse to death by the sheltered shore.

--Anonymous

* * *

TODAY

   What you do today that is worthwhile, inspires others to act
at some future time.

--Marcus Garvey

* * *

TOKENISM

   All token blacks have the same experience. I have been
pointed at as a solution to things that have not begun to be
solved, because pointing at us token blacks eases the conscience
of millions and I think this is dreadfully wrong.

--Leontyne Price

* * *

TOMB

I would like them to write on my tomb, 'He has lived for peace, and has died for principles.

--Anwar el-Sadat

* * *

TRADE

We must fight for trade-not just aid! We must fight for economic reciprocity-not just social generosity.

--Jesse Jackson

* * *

TRAVEL

Travel is the great source of true wisdom.

--Afro American

* * *

TROUBLE

I'm so glad Trouble don't last always; . . .
Hallelujah, I'm so glad trouble don't last always.

--Black Spiritual

_____

All my troubles will soon be over with,
Soon be over with.
All over the world.

--Black Spiritual

_____

Nobody knows de trouble I see
Nobody knows but Jesus
Nobody knows de trouble I see
Glory, Halleluyah.

                                        --Black Spiritual

                    *   *   *

TRUTH

Truth and the morning become light with time.

                                        --African Proverb
                    _____

Truth crushed to earth shall rise again.

                                        --Martin Luther King Jr.
                    _____

Truth is like Gold: keep it locked up and you will find it
exactly as you first put it away.

                                        --African Proverb
                    _____

I still believe that standing up for the truth of God is the
greatest thing in the world.

                                        --Martin Luther King Jr.

                    *   *   *

TRYING

When you try all you can, try some more.

                                        --Black Maxim

                    *   *   *

U

UNCOMPROMISING

All or nothing.

--Walter White

*   *   *

UNDERGROUND RAILROAD

I Nebber run my train
off the track An' I Nebber
los a passenger.

--Harriet Tubman

*   *   *

UNEMPLOYED

If the unemployed could eat plans and promises, they would be
able to spend the winter on the Riviera.

--W.E.B. Dubois

*   *   *

UNIQUENESS

Certainly I'm unique in country music. But each of us is unique, I just happen to have a permanent tan.

--Charlie Pride

* * *

UNITY

All for one, one for all.

--Alexandre Dumas pére

* * *

UPPERCLASS

The Negro upperclass wants to know why I am out here struggling in behalf of the oppressed, exploited Negro of the south when I could isolate myself from them like they do and become wealthy by keeping quiet on such disturbing subjects. This I have found, would not be true of me. What I earn doesn't help my people that much. I have relatives in the south struggling to make a living.

--Paul Robeson

* * *

V

VANITY

I myself consider myself to be the most important figure in
the world.

--Idi Amin

* * *

VICES

Our vices and our degradation are ever arrayed against us, but
our virtues are passed by unnoticed.

--Freedom's Journal

* * *

VICISSITUDES

A smooth sea never made a skillful mariner.

--Afro American

* * *

VIGILANCE

If you watch your pot, your food will not burn.

--African Proverb

* * *

VIOLENCE

Violence is as American as cherry pie.

* * *

VIRTUE

Virtue is better than wealth.

--African Proverb

* * *

VOODOO

I am the prophet of the dusky race,
The poet of wild Africa. Behold
The midnight vision brooding in my face!
      Come near me,
      And hear me,
While from my lips the words of Fate are told
A black and terrible memory masters me;
The shadow and substance of deep wrong.
You know the past, hear now what is to be,
      From the midnight land,
      Over sea and sand,
From the green jungle hear my voodoo song:

A tropic heat is in my bubbling veins,
Quintessence of all savagery is mine,
The lust of ages ripens in my veins,
          And burns
          And burns
Like venom sap within a noxious vine.

Was I a heathen? Ay, I was-am still
A fetich worshipper; but I was free!
To loiter or to wander at my will;
          To leap and dance,
          To hurl my lance,
And breathe the air of savage liberty.
You drew me to a higher life you say,
Ah, drove me with the lash of slavery!
And I unmindful? Every cursed day
          of pain
          and chain
Roars like a torrent in my memory.

                              --Maurice Thompson

                  *   *   *

                      VOTE

        If he knows enough to be hanged, he knows enough to
vote.

                          --Frederick Douglass

                  *   *   *

W

WAITING

We have waited for more than 340 years for our constitutional and God given rights.

--Martin Luther King Jr.

_____

The American Negro has been waiting upon voluntary action since 1876. He has found what other Americans have discovered: voluntary action has to be sparked by something stronger than prayers, patience and lamentations. If the thirteen colonies had waited for voluntary action by England, this land today would be a part of the British Commonwealth.

--Roy Wilkins

* * *

WAR

There are no warlike people- just warlike leaders.

--Ralph Bunche

* * *

WEAK

The weakest is always in the wrong.

--Creole Slave Proverb

* * *

WEALTH

With wealth one wins a woman.

--African Proverb

Wealth will give no true happiness or satisfaction. Pleasure
is only a shadow of happiness. The secret of life is to
accomplish your life's purpose.

--Muhammad Ali

I would prefer to be honestly wealthy, than miserably poor.

--Marcus Garvey

* * *

WELFARE

I can tell by your knees you've been eating welfare cheese.

--Black Saying

* * *

WHITE HOUSE

The White House is a house for white people.

--Eddie Carlin Jr.

* * *

WHITE MAN

It is a peculiar thing that almost without exception, all distinguished white men have been favourably disposed towards their black breathren.

--Samuel Coleridge Taylor

* * *

WHITE SUPREMACY

The whole doctrine of white supremacy comes from Europe.

--James Baldwin

* * *

WICKED

A wicked man is afraid of his own memory.

--Afro American

* * *

WIFE

If you want peace in the house do what your wife wants.

--African Proverb

A good wife and health are a man's best wealth.

--Afro American

* * *

WILD

I am just wild about Harry and Harry's wild about me.

--Eubie Blake

* * *

WISDOM

Wisdom is not in the eye, but in the head.

--African Proverb

* * *

WOMAN

Beautiful woman, beautiful trouble.

--African Proverb

_____

While man can boast of great physical strength, skill and bull dog courage, woman carries in her weak frame a moral courage very seldom found among men.

--American Baptist

_____

No real man can do without her.

--Marcus Garvey

_____

Woman cannot enjoy equality and chivalry at the same time.

--Jack Johnson

_____

Whatever a woman's talents or rights may be, her natural place is the home.

--Jack Johnson

_____

A man can survive a heated quarrel with a woman, but what takes the heat out of a man is her determination to warm it over, every day, for a week afterward.

--Leonard Massenburge

_____

Nobody ever helped me into carriages or over mud puddles or gives me a best place. And ain't I a woman.

--Sojourner Truth

_____

If a woman speaks two words, take one and leave the other.

--African Proverb

_____

Don't want no woman puttin' sugar in my tea
Don't want no woman puttin' sugar in my tea
'Cause I'm evil, 'fraid she might poison me.

--Black Saying

_____

A woman who knows how to cook is mighty pretty.

--Black Saying

*   *   *

WOMEN

The major thing I have learned is that women are the backbone of America's political organizations.

--Shirley Chisholm

_____

A race, no less than a nation, is prosperous in proportion to
the intelligence of its women.

--M.A. Majors

I like all women who are beautiful.

--Adam Clayton Powell Jr.

*   *   *

WOMEN'S LIBERATION

Black women worked their fingers to the bone and Black men
were lynched to pay homage to white ladies. Hence, it's hard to
conceive how these very women could expect Blacks to empathize
with members of the most privileged class cults in U.S. History:
sacred white womanhood.

--Alvin F. Poussaint

*   *   *

WORK

If you want to be the best . . . not just the black best.
. . . You've got to work harder than anybody else.

--Sammy Davis Jr.

A man's bread and butter is only assured when he works for it.

--Marcus Garvey

*   *   *

WORSHIP

As the physical body needs renewal, so must the spiritual body be renewed. Worship provides the spiritual renewal necessary for a healthy spiritual life.

--Martin Luther King Jr.

* * *

WRATH

Liberty came to the Freedman not in mercy, but in wrath, not word choice, but by military necessity, not by the generous action of the people among whom they were to live, and whose goodwill was essential to the success of the measure, but by strangers.

--Frederick Douglass

* * *

WRITERS

I moved to Europe in 1948 because I was trying to become a writer and couldn't find in my surroundings, in my own country, a certain stamina, a certain corroboration that I needed. For example, no one ever told me that Alexandre Dumas was a mulatto. No one told me that Pushkin was black. As far as I knew when I was very young there'd never been anything. . . . As far as I knew, which is much more important, there'd never been anything called a black writer.

--James Baldwin

Writers are extremely important in a country, whether or not the country knows it.

--James Baldwin

* * *

WRITING

In my writing I am proud to feature their concerns, their troubles as well as their joys. It is my privilege to present Negroes not as curiosities but as people.

--Gwendolyn Brooks

* * *

Y

<u>YESTERDAY</u>

To heck with yesterday! What are we gonna do tomorrow.

--Ada (Bricktop) Smith

*   *   *

INDEX

About the Author

Donnie E. (Don) Wilson was the former County Attorney for Shelby County, Tennessee. Mr. Wilson is a member of the Bars of the District of Columbia, the Commonwealth of Pennsylvania, the State of Tennessee, as well as the United States Supreme Court and numerous other federal and state courts. He received his Bachelor of Arts Degree in History and English from the University of Arkansas, Pine Bluff. He received his Juris Doctorate Degree from Southern University Law School. Born in Pine Bluff, Arkansas, he resides with his wife Antoinette in Memphis, Tennessee.

0-595-32621-8